CHRISTMAS
In Oklahoma

CHRISTMAS
In Oklahoma

Past and Present

by
Linda Kennedy Rosser

WESTERN HERITAGE BOOKS

Mistletoe, the design on the cover, an ancient holiday symbol, was found in abundance in this young state. It was named the state flower although it is a parasite and not a flower at all.

For information, write
Bobwhite Publications,
P.O. Box 14641, Oklahoma City,
Oklahoma 73113.

This book is dedicated
to
Rex

Preface

No matter how primitive, lonely, or strange the conditions, Christmas produces the deepest of human emotions. At no time and place in American history has a broader range of circumstances existed for celebrating Christmas than in Indian Territory and Oklahoma Territory, beginning with the arrival of missionaries among the Five Civilized Tribes in the late 1820's, until the Twin Territories merged to form the state of Oklahoma in 1907, following the tumultuous Boomer movement bringing thousands of settlers to stake claims in Oklahoma country, *the beautiful land*. True stories of Indians, missionaries, Cavalry officers, pioneers, and frontier townspeople at Christmas reflect the patchwork quality of the heritage of this young state celebrating its seventy-fifth anniversary Diamond Jubilee.

Christmas in Oklahoma of 1982 is a blending of the traditions of the hearty people who *went pioneering*, of immigrants from foreign lands—Czechs, Germans, Poles, Italians, British, Irish, Mexicans, Greeks, Lebanese—of blacks, at last able to own a homestead, and of the Indians who continue to inhabit the hills and plains. The people are as varied as the land, from wooded hills in the east, through rolling prairie plains of the midlands, to the high arid plains of the west. Christmas customs have been adapted to the broad spectrum of lifestyles, from frontier towns and cities to sophisticated metropolises, and from cowboys and farmers to *city folks*.

Oklahoma continues to be *the beautiful land*, as full of promise today as it was with the Land Run of 1889, and still attracting hoards of newcomers. Christmas time in Oklahoma is a time to celebrate the uniqueness of our past, the richness of our present, and the promise of our future.

Merry Christmas!
Linda Kennedy Rosser

ACKNOWLEDGEMENTS

My grateful thanks to these people for their help! All the families and individuals who shared their stories and recipes; the librarians and staff at the Oklahoma Historical Society, the Newspaper Division, Reference Library, and, particularly, the Archives and Manuscript Division; Paul Lambert and Kenny Franks of the Oklahoma Heritage Association; the Oklahoma Department of Libraries; Ruby Cranor in the History Room of the Bartlesville Public Library; the Western History Collections of the University of Oklahoma Library; Vera Bremseth and Pauline Lane, volunteers with the 1889er Harn Museum and Gardens; Charlotte Jenkens at the Stephens County Historical Museum; Ralph Jones at the Overholser Mansion; Lucy Stansberry at the Elk City Old Town Museum; the U.S. Field Artillery Museum at Fort Sill; Jody Yancey at the Omniplex; Don Green and Stan Hoig at Central State University for urging me on; and Michelle Lefebvre, Jack Conn and the Oklahoma Diamond Jubilee Commission for recognizing this as a Diamond Jubilee Project.

More thanks to: Dorothy Kennedy, Marta McGee, Barbara Stanfield, Betty Lou Fritsche, Sybil Peters, Linda Massad, Dorthlynn Gaddis, Edith Rainey, Peggy Haynes, and Ron Rosser.

Special thanks to: Judy Samter, Alyson Stanfield, and Jill Hunting for assistance with illustrations, design, and layout.

CONTENTS

Part I CHRISTMAS IN THE TWIN TERRITORIES

WITH THE INDIANS

ON THE FRONTIER

PERMANENT SETTLERS CELEBRATE

Part II MEMORIES AND TRADITIONS

MEMORIES OF CHRISTMASES AFTER STATEHOOD

TODAY'S TRADITIONS ARE TOMORROW'S MEMORIES

Part III CHRISTMAS DELIGHTS
FROM THE KITCHEN

CHRISTMAS IN THE TWIN TERRITORIES

A little blackjack oak with shiny brown leaves, strung with popcorn and tinfoil and topped with a tin star, suited pioneers who couldn't find an evergreen.

With The Indians

AMONG THE DEAR CHEROKEES

"Reaching the mission at twilight, we emerged from the dense forest, and our ears were saluted by the delightful sound of the church bell—a church bell in a heathen land! It thrilled my inmost soul and stirred up feeling which I shall never forget."

The young missionary looked around at the log cabins making up the village of Fort Smith, Arkansas. This town on the edge of the frontier was a far cry from the colonial town in Connecticut where he grew up. Henry R. Wilson was committed to helping his fellow man by answering the call of the Presbyterian Mission Board to come to the mission established in Indian Territory four years ago. As he bedded down for a night's rest in the rustic cabin provided for travelers, he wondered what Christmas would be like among the Indians that Christmas of 1832.

The next morning, rested and excited, Henry Wilson prepared to join the Reverend Cephas Washburn, founder of Dwight Mission, located in the Cherokee Nation west, more than thirty miles from Fort Smith. Arrangements for a guide and horses had been made for the last leg of Wilson's journey deep into Indian Territory. They set out through the trackless forest, and periodically an open hillside reminded Henry of the hills he loved back in New England. Sounds of the horse hooves crushing the frozen leaves were the only interruption in the quiet forest.

In preparation for his position as Reverend Washburn's assistant, Wilson had undoubtedly studied government plans to move Indians from the southern part of the United States to Indian Territory, land which was part of the Louisiana Purchase. Most of the Cherokees he would meet had come from Georgia, and the mission had been established to help them adjust to this substitute homeland, as well as teach them the ways of the white man's civilization. Other religious groups were planning missions and schools: Methodists, Lutherans, Baptists, Quakers, Catholics, and Moravians.

As the party neared Dwight Mission, the December sun was low in the western sky, and the density of the forest had further shortened the winter day severely. In the twilight, they emerged from the woods and heard the church bell at the mission. Deeply touched, Wilson knew the memory of that moment would last a lifetime. It was Saturday, December 21, 1832. The church bell signaled a large group of converted Indians and missionaries from neighboring stations to gather for prayer in preparation for communion the following day.

After the long horseback ride, the young missionary was tired and hungry, but he also was anxious to join the congregation assembled in the schoolhouse being used temporarily for church services until a chapel could be built. Wilson took only a few minutes for refreshment before he approached the schoolhouse. Years later he would recall that there "I had my first interview with the Reverend Washburn and the dear Cherokees whom he had converted."

"When I entered," he wrote, "they were singing a hymn in the Cherokee language. Never before did music appear half so sweet to me; the language is music itself. The air was a sweet one, and the deep feeling of devotion with which it was sung rendered it truly refreshing."

What a greeting for a young man who had traveled halfway across the continent to help his fellow man, and what a memorable Christmas season for one who had always spent family Christmases in New England amid longstanding traditions.

As the church service progressed, an old, gray-haired Indian arose. His face seemed to beam with love and gratitude as he poured forth his feelings in a manner which Wilson had never witnessed before. "While I could not understand a word," he recalled, "I felt deeply moved to see one who had so often led his countrymen to war now leading them to the throne of Jesus Christ."

Wilson's introduction to missionary life among the red men of the forest began with a Sabbath day filled with prayer, conference meetings, and the Lord's Supper; all of this was a preliminary to Christmas services, which he soon learned would be held at the home of Colonel Walter Webber. Reverend Washburn explained that although not converted to Christianity, Colonel Webber was one of the head-men, or chiefs, of the Cherokees and had invited the missionaries and Christianized Indians to spend the holiday at his place near the Arkansas River, more than 60 miles northwest of the mission.

Shuddering at the thought of another excursion so soon after his strenuous journey from the East, Wilson nevertheless prepared for another adventure. Twenty-five or 30 men joined the two missionaries for the trip, which would take most of two days. Late in the first afternoon, they stopped on the trail to set up temporary camp. Ravenous after the long, cold ride through forests and swamps, the weary travelers removed supplies from their saddlebags for a frugal meal while several men gathered firewood. With log fires built, the men gathered around them to keep warm. They made the fires large enough to burn through most of the night.

This was the first time in his life that Henry Wilson had slept on the ground with the broad canopy of heaven for his covering. He tried to sleep, but the cold and the strangeness of the circumstances made it extremely difficult for him to relax.

The next morning they resumed their journey, some of the men walking while others rode. The hilly and wooded terrain of that part of Indian Territory was the western edge of the Ozark Mountains and not unlike the land some of these Indians had left in Georgia, North Carolina, and Tennessee. The Cherokees, along with the Choctaws, Creeks, Chickasaws, and

Seminoles, were called the Five Civilized Tribes because, prior to their removal from the southern regions of the United States, many had adopted their white neighbors' lifestyles. Some were farmers and businessmen; some wore *civilized* clothing and were well educated; and a few of the wealthiest tribal leaders owned slaves and had brought them west, making them the first black residents of Oklahoma.

When they reached their destination, Henry Wilson was surprised to see more than a hundred Indians. Men, women, and children had gathered to celebrate Christmas together. As there were no buildings large enough to hold the multitude, they held daytime meetings outdoors, and at night they gathered in small groups in the warmth of cabins in the immediate vicinity. Reverend Washburn, Reverend Wilson, and other missionaries worked diligently to convert more of the Indians during the three days and nights of the Christmas season. Even the genial host, Colonel Webber, had *his heart opened* and was converted to Christianity. The missionaries deeply hoped their work would make the life of the Indians better.

Thirty years later, Henry Wilson reflected on the memories of his first Christmas as a missionary in the Indian Territory: "This was the happiest Christmas I ever spent, though far from home and friends and destitute of the luxuries and comforts to which I have become accustomed."

Adapted from The Tulsa Daily World, December 22, 1929.

NOT ENOUGH TO GO AROUND

At the close of the Civil War, A. T. Dickerman found himself without a job after four years as a civilian scout and trader among the Indians. He spoke three languages fluently, knew all the grades of fur, from opossum to buffalo, and could build a house with no tools other than an ax, auger, saw, and fro. To three merchants from Oswego, Kansas, he seemed a perfect choice to build and manage a trading post they planned to finance in the Cherokee Nation. One of the partners, N. F. Carr, had gained the right to do business there through his marriage to a beautiful quarter-blood Cherokee girl whose father was a well-educated interpreter.

Two wagons of supplies, three men, and a 14-year-old boy left Oswego for the site selected on the Big Caney River where the old Black Dog Indian trail crossed the river (about one mile from where Bartlesville eventually would be established). They were surprised to be greeted by two large bands of Osage Indians, the Big Hill band, 1000 strong, camped a half-mile above, and the Black Dog band a mile below. Within two hours the traders had distributed both loads of goods, reserving enough to last the post a few days.

After the men had laid the foundation for the trading post building, Dickerman and the boy, Johnny Kaho, were left to complete the construction. It was mid-December, 1867. All Christmas Eve day the veteran scout worked on the framework, cutting, hauling, and erecting logs. He enlisted six of the Indians to help *raise* the house.

Early Christmas morning he began the work of riving boards to cover the building. About 9:00 o'clock he looked up to see the Indians—men, women, and children—coming into camp, all dressed in their "Sunday-go-to-meeting-clothes." The men wore their best blankets and were bedecked with paint, earbobs, and feathers. The women had ribbons in their *strands*, and their garters and moccasins were covered with beads. They surrounded the camp and stood watching Dickerman split boards. "They were perfectly decorous until about 11 o'clock," recalled the trader years later, "when Johnny, having eating chills, begged me to allow him to get our dinner."

He told the impatient boy that it would never do, that if they sat down to eat their limited provisions without inviting the chiefs and braves, they would insult the Indians. Johnny took it rather hard and complained loudly about the Indians beating him out of his Christmas dinner.

About noon old Conseoceta (meaning "good apples"), chief counselor to Chief Big Hill Joseph Pawnemopaskee, came up to Dickerman and said, "My friend, don't you know that this is God's day?"

"Yes," he replied, "every day is God's day."

"But don't you know that on this day all the great white men make a great feast and invite all their friends? We are all hungry for bread and coffee. Ain't you going to cook a big dinner and ask us all to eat with you?"

The experienced scout looked around at the crowd, which he estimated at 2000, and knew it was impossible. He explained to Conseoceta that some white people made a big feast, but others on Christmas fasted and worked all day just as hard as they could, and that he was one of those. The Indian rejoined his band, and they continued to watch. The weather was very warm for Christmas, and, because he wanted to finish the boards that day, Dickerman was really exerting himself and did not stop for rest. After two more hours the Indian approached again and said, "My friend, are you not getting hungry? You look tired, and the sweat is just dripping off your face."

"No," was the reply. "I never get hungry on Christmas day. I am full of God clear up to my chin, and if I should swallow anything, it would choke me."

Conseoceta said no more, and about 3:00 o'clock the Indians began to go away. By sundown all had gone except an old brave, Pahapa, and another elderly Indian. Johnny was instructed to start supper, and Dickerman turned to the two remaining Indians and said, "Now the sun is gone. Christmas is gone. We can eat."

"O, my father," Pahapa said, "I know what is the matter. You haven't got but just a little handful of coffee and just a little handful of flour, and all of the Indians would have eaten it all up and you wouldn't have had any."

Adapted from the Oswego Democrat, December 22, 1911.

CUSTER'S CHRISTMAS IN I.T.

It was just a month before Christmas in 1868 when General George A. Custer marched out of newly established Camp Supply in Indian Territory to attack and capture the village of Black Kettle's Cheyennes on the Washita River. They spent the next month taking the prisoners back to camp and marching to Fort Cobb, accompanied by General Philip Sheridan. There they attempted to force the Indians to stay on the reservations.

Christmas came, and a soldier in the Seventh Cavalry wrote in his diary what it was like being a frontier soldier at Christmas time:

"Near Fort Cobb, Indian Territory, Dec. 25, 1868. The morning is cool and windy and very dusty. Today is Christmas Day and I have only two hard tacks for my dinner and a quart of bean soup that a hog would not eat if he were starving. This is the kind of a dinner I have to sit down to today, alright...."

Adapted from "Christmases Ago-" by Stan Hoig.

WHITE DOVES FLUTTERING

A merry company of young folks, comprising all the little people at the Cheyenne and Arapahoe Agency, gathered at the residence of Captain Connell on the Saturday evening before Christmas in 1891. The captain's daughters Lillie and Ella had issued printed invitations, and a large group responded. After all the children assembled, Santa Claus was announced and the parlor doors thrown open. The expectant boys and girls admired the Christmas tree loaded down with its precious burden of gifts and trinkets. It sparkled and flashed with twinkling lights and dangling pendants. The youngsters rushed into the room, and, after feasting their eyes to their hearts' content, they stripped the beautiful tree of its treats and divided them among themselves.

When Mrs. Connell brought in the goodies, candies, cakes, and sweetmeats*, they disappeared more quickly than they had appeared. Attracting the most attention was the Christmas cake made by Mrs. Putt—a handsomely iced cake with the magic words, "Merry Christmas," written on top in scarlet letters. This masterpiece was capped off by a pair of white doves fluttering over a nest in the center of the cake.

It did not take long for the young people to devour the wonderful cake, and then they turned to games. The jolly, romping crowd had full sway and kept the fun alive until it was time for them to go home.

Under the guidance of their parents, the young revelers were soon at home abed— there to dream of Santa Claus and his wonderful team a-prancing and a-dancing while the busy old fellow was sliding down and up the chimneys of the Agency to arrange new surprises for them when they opened their sleepy eyes in the morning.

*Sweetmeats refers to any of a variety of sweet dainties of confectionery, including candied fruits, sugar-covered nuts, bon-bons, or sticks of candy.

CHRISTMAS BOXES FROM KIND FRIENDS IN THE EAST

Missionaries were not the only ones to introduce the Indians in the Territories to the customs of Christmas. The United States government established Indian Agencies to provide food, supplies, technical training, and medical aid to the various tribes throughout the Territories. Each agency employed a Field Matron to teach the Indian women sewing and cooking, to assist them with nutrition and health, and to visit their homes and build friendly relationships.

In southwestern Oklahoma Territory, not far from the military outpost of Fort Sill, was the Kiowa Agency. Along with the Wichita, Caddo, and Comanche tribes, the Kiowas had inhabited these plains and rocky hills long before exploration by outsiders.

Lauretta Ballew was Field Matron at the Rainy Mountain Mission on the Kiowa Reservation, and as part of her duties she was required to file quarterly reports on her work with the Indians. From these reports it is possible to tell how the Plains Indians celebrated Christmas during the later part of the nineteenth century.

In 1896 Miss Ballew worked for days decorating a Christmas tree, which she placed in Immanuel Chapel at Rainy Mountain Mission. Friends in the East had sent supplies for the event, so the Christmas tree was loaded with 380 presents for the Indians. The tiny chapel was filled to capacity with people on Christmas Eve, and the Kiowas gazed at the beautiful tree. As the gifts were distributed one by one, each Indian murmured, "Ah-ho, ah-ho" (thank you). In addition to these gifts, there were two large barrels near the tree brimming over with bags of candy, one bag for each person in the chapel.

"Is it not wonderful how our friends in the East have remembered us?" one of the Indians remarked.

Miss Ballew felt certain that if these Eastern friends could have looked in on the pleasant sight and seen the gratitude of the Indians, they would have felt more than repaid for their work.

Little Indian girls clutched their new dolls while one boy blew his horn as Dr. C. Ross Hume's wife took their picture in front of the elaborately decorated tree at the Episcopal Chapel, Riverside Indian Church, near Anadarko, O.T., in 1898. (Photo courtesy Western History Collections, University of Oklahoma Library, and The Anadarko Philomathic Museum.)

The crowd was so large the night of the Christmas tree that it was obvious Immanuel Chapel needed to be enlarged, so a collection was taken for the project. Indians as well as Agency employees gave donations totaling 10 dollars. One Kiowa woman's face shone with gladness when she was able to give 50 cents. Accepting this generous gift, Lauretta recalled an-

other gift this woman once had offered her, a horse. When Lauretta had refused to accept the horse, the woman had seemed hurt and said, "I can't understand how anyone would refuse a gift." The following winter the rejected horse had died, and the Field Matron was told by the woman that the horse had died because Lauretta had not taken it. This Christmas Miss Ballew gladly accepted the 50-cent offering from the old woman; she had learned her lesson in refusing the previous gift.

By 1900, four years later, Lauretta saw many changes in the skills and living habits of the Kiowas served by Rainy Mountain Mission. Most lived in houses, 135 families, but some still held to their ancient lifestyle, preferring tepees. However, this only included 20 families. During the fall of 1900 Miss Ballew visited those vastly different types of dwellings as she attended 12 births and five deaths.

That was a busy fall supervising sewing activities of the Kiowa women, and it was with pride that Lauretta reported the completion of 27 quilts and 161 garments. Before teaching them to sew, she first had to instruct them in how to cut out patterns, so during that autumn she assisted them in cutting out 19 patterns for *civilized garments*. To prepare for the cold winter winds which would sweep across the plains, Miss Ballew helped many of the women clean and remodel their houses.

As Christmas approached, the Indians made presents for each other: trinkets, bows and arrows, moccasins, and *old-time dolls*. As in years past, *kind friends in the East* sent Christmas boxes and barrels of candy to help the Indians have a merry Christmas.

As the Kiowas gathered in the enlarged Immanuel Chapel at Rainy Mountain Mission for the Christmas tree in 1900, they did not know it would be the last Christmas they would celebrate with their reservation intact. The following June would bring the beginning of lotteries dividing the land for individual ownership and pioneer settlement.

Ironically, Lauretta Ballew began her quarterly report that year by stating, "The quarter ends with a very Merry Christmas and prospects of a happy New Year."

AT THE SAC AND FOX AGENCY

A typical Indian Agency contained facilities similar to those at the Sac and Fox Agency in the central part of the Territories. Four large brick buildings provided classrooms for the school children and dormitory space for single women employed at the Agency: the cook, seamstress, matron, laundress, and teachers. Two stockade homes at the Sac and Fox Agency were inhabited by the Agent's family and Tribal Chief Moses Keokuk and his family. The Indians held meetings in the council house, and supplies were stored in the commissary. Those arrested by the Indian police were promptly thrown into the log calaboose—better known today as the jail. Frame store buildings were well stocked by licensed Indian traders purveying the assorted supplies needed by tribespeople, villagers, and travelers. Besides the Agent, other employees lived in homes provided by the government, including the physician, blacksmith, Agency clerks, Indian police, and the Agency farmer, who taught agricultural techniques to the Indians.

One church served the community, The Only Way Baptist Church. It was shared by whites, Indians, and mixed-bloods. The Agency blacksmith's son recalled Christmas at The Only Way Baptist Church by saying, "Our kind of Christmas was entirely new to them."

When he arrived at the Agency, he was amazed to find that Indian children had not always had Christmas trees with gifts and special treats. His first Christmas there he watched with keen interest as he sat in the crowded church and the *wonderful*

Indian children marched around the candle-lighted tree on their way out at the end of the program. Each child received a large bag made from mosquito netting which contained a shiny red apple, a popcorn ball, chewing gum, lots of candy, and a large orange (a novelty in Indian country).

"It did wonders to us when we saw how happy they were," recalled the blacksmith's boy. "Their eyes sparkled, their faces beamed, and they jabbered in Sac and Fox and giggled and squeaked."

Adapted from Oklahoma Chronicles, "The Only Way Church and the Sac and Fox Indians," by R. Morton House, Vol. XLIII (1965).

SEARCH FOR SANTA AT CHILOCCO INDIAN SCHOOL

Although suggestions of Christmas were rife for weeks at Chilocco Indian School, located in far northern Oklahoma Territory near the border of Kansas, the holiday season of 1905 did not open officially until the evening of December 22nd. That night all the performers in the Christmas exercises held a dress rehearsal in the chapel for the benefit of the little tots. Chilocco had a wide range of ages among the boys and girls who were boarding students at the school, which had been established in 1882. The curriculum offered older students above the elementary level more advanced courses than most schools and academies in I.T. and O.T. Formal education in the Territories frequently was a joint effort of the government, mission-

ary societies, and national councils of the Five Civilized Tribes.

As Christmas of 1905 approached, boys enrolled in carpentry classes practiced their skills by building stage settings and backdrops for the special Christmas program, with particular attention given to sets for the Cantata entitled "A Christmas Crusade, or Santa Claus in the Klondike Gold Regions" (a popular subject for dramatics in 1905). Young ladies in dressmaking classes spent hours sewing costumes for participants in the exercises.

While girls in cooking class prepared special refreshments for the holidays, members of both the orchestra and the second band rehearsed their numbers.

The stage of the Friends' Mission School, established in 1872, was decorated with garlands and Christmas messages at Christmas of 1874. J. W. Kirk was Superintendent of the school, which served the Wyandotte Indians and was located near the present town of Wyandotte (called Grand River until 1894). The name later was changed to Seneca Indian School after its takeover by the U. S. government. The side walls of the large, cheerful schoolroom contained garlands and messages reading "Merry Christmas" and "Joy to the World." (Photo courtesy Oklahoma Historical Society.)

Irene Dardene practiced her recitation, "Two Little Stockings," and Grace Miller memorized "Christmas Night in the Quarters." Boys in the dormitory were getting sick of hearing the Seymorian Polka on Andre Moya's cornet by the time he finally performed his solo, and the refrain of "The Good Night Song" was well known by all the girls sharing a dorm with

Haydee Iron Thunder and the five other girls planning to sing it at the December 23rd program.

The evening finally arrived, and the program was "rendered with fine effect," according to reports in the *Indian School Journal*, before a large and appreciative audience of children, parents, and friends. The first half included the musical numbers, recitations, and a tableau of "Shepherds Watching Their Flock." (A tableau was a popular form of entertainment in homes and schools in which costumed actors simply posed in a fixed scene, holding very still for several minutes as if in a picture.)

The crowning feature of the evening was the dramatic presentation, or Cantata. It opened with the principal characters, Francesca and Wahnita, hunting through the woods for Santa Claus. Jack Rabbit and the children came to their assistance in the next scene. During the second act, entitled "Witches' Brew," witches gave tokens to the search party to aid in finding Santa. The last act produced knights and fairies, who joined in the search, and the final scene depicted poor Santa Claus being held prisoner by Old Zero and his gnomes. Finally the jolly old man was rescued from his abductors by the knights and fairies, and Christmas was saved. The Cantata closed with a tableau by the entire cast.

Reaction to the performance was understandably enthusiastic: "The fairies, gnomes and other children of the forest presented a picture of gayety [sic] indeed, while Jack Rabbit made quite a hit, or perhaps we should say jump."

On Christmas Eve there were Christmas trees in the various homes on the grounds of the boarding school, and Santa had to "hustle around lively" to get to all of them. The following morning the usual Sunday School was replaced with a song service followed at noon by a huge Christmas dinner. Students could barely eat they were so busy talking about the wonderful presents delivered by Santa the night before.

A public band concert on Christmas afternoon attracted a large number of neighbors, who enjoyed Strauss waltzes, marches, a saxaphone quartet, and other classical and popular selections.

The final day of the holiday, a Monday, began with a morning dress parade and concluded with an afternoon football game in Arkansas City, Kansas, just over the border.

"Upon the whole, a happier Christmas could never be imagined," was the final assessment of Christmas, 1905, at Chilocco Indian School, Indian Territory.

ON THE FRONTIER

CHRISTMAS AT OLD FORT SILL

General Sheridan and his men were fed up with the floods, cold weather, poor food, and inadequate shelter at Fort Cobb that Christmas of 1868; so two days after Christmas he sent 40 cavalrymen, under the command of Colonel Benjamin H. Grierson, to reconnoiter the Medicine Bluff Creek area south of Fort Cobb. Grey Leggins, a Comanche guide, accompanied them as an interpreter, and a journalist went along to record what happened.

They returned with good reports of ample pure water from mountain streams, prairies of nutritious grass, plenty of timber, and rich soil. From the summit above the creek, they had been able to see Mount Scott eight miles to the northwest. General Sheridan agreed this would be the perfect spot for a permanent post to pacify the Plains Indians, protect Agencies in the area, and keep peace among the various tribes. Not until July 2, 1868, was the post officially named Fort Sill, and by that time Grierson had become post commander.

Grierson and his men spent the next few years building permanent military buildings. At Christmas time, 1871, Grierson wrote his wife Alice, "Mrs. Carlton has sent you a chair for a Christmas present. It is an army chair made of black walnut, has a cushion seat which is covered with green damask striped with yellow....The back is the same material. The chair folds up and is the prettiest folding chair I ever saw. It must have cost, I should judge, at least 10$. I returned your thanks in as appropriate manner as possible. I very much wish you were now here to sit in it."

The party on Christmas night "went off first rate." They had a small, but very pretty Christmas tree, and the rooms above the parlor used for dancing were decorated with pictures Grierson had hung on the walls for the occasion.

Although Alice Grierson spent Christmas of 1871 away from her husband, she described every gift on the family tree in Chicago, including cornucopias filled with candy, picture books, wax dolls, and a box of blocks. Because the children's papa was out in Indian Territory, Alice took his place, dressing as *Santa Claus in petticoats*.

Fort Sill by the 1880s had become a pleasant military village. Stone buildings of grey limestone quarried southeast of the post lined the four sides of the common square; well-dressed men and women attended the church and frequented the general store; and a lively social life existed, especially at holiday time.

Men assigned to military posts continued their duties even at Christmas time. Lieutenant Glasford, inspector in the employ of the Signal Corps, made a tour of

Christmas at Fort Sill for this military man and his daughters included a large ever-green tree festooned with cornucopias, glass ornaments, baskets, and, at the top, two American flags. Dolls always were the favorite gift for little girls, especially those who received two. (Photo courtesy U.S. Army Field Artillery Museum.)

inspection during the bitterly cold days that preceded Christmas of 1881. He was pleased with the business procedures at Anadarko's telegraph office, but he perhaps was more pleased to attend a dance at the Wichita Social Club while he was in town. Much to his regret, he could not stay for the big event of the season, the Calico Ball. More than 100 invitations had

been issued for the festive Christmas ball being planned by the Wichita Social Club.

In November of 1886 two young women arrived at Fort Sill from Dallas, Texas: Marion Brown and her friend Carrie Shumard. They planned an extended visit through the holidays with Carrie's mother at the fort. Twenty-nine and single, Marion had not been healthy during the fall, so her father, a newspaper publisher and mayor of Dallas, decided the dry climate of Fort Sill would be restorative. The social life of the garrison was so active that Marion had little time to worry about her health.

During her three-month stay Marion exchanged many letters with her family (preserved in the John Henry Brown Collection at the University of Texas Archives). Her accounts of Christmas at Fort Sill shed an interesting light on life there.

Many eligible young officers were available—and anxious—to escort the two new arrivals for cards, dancing, and socializing. Other interesting citizens of the community, like the elderly Dr. Morse K. Taylor, an outstanding army surgeon, were charmed by the two young women and their interest in the history of Indian Territory.

Early one evening in December a group of ladies gathered at the home of Mrs. Pearson, one of the fort's social leaders, to make bags for Christmas candies and banners for decoration. The gents were not allowed until the ladies had been working for an hour, probably to insure that work was uninterrupted. Everyone had fun cutting and conversing. At 10:00 o'clock Mrs. Pearson served a supper, and afterwards all joined in a game of gunnin. Marion's escort for the evening was Lieutenant Crane, whose attentions were sought both by Marion and Carrie.

The following week the two friends entertained 10 guests at a "splendid" dinner at which the music, company, and meal were so enjoyable that they decided to make it a weekly event. As Christmas drew

closer, another lively event was planned, a *hop* (or dance). "The hop was a perfect success," Marion wrote home. "As it was informal we only danced until 12 o'clock. Carrie and I were lovely in our sateens. After the dancing was over it was announced that every one was invited to go over to Capt. King's and have refreshments. The supper was elegant, the host & hostess cordial and before we realized the fact it was after 1 o'clock."

There was no shortage of ideas for social activities at Fort Sill, with music, cards, dancing, and plans for a Christmas *grand hop*. Perhaps Marion's sister Clara had no idea how busy life at a military outpost was when she wrote suggesting a Christmas entertainment called a *Christmas pie*. She described how to fill a very large dishpan with sawdust, then insert a small gift for each person attending. Each should be accompanied by some funny little pun or poetry about the recipient. The final step in preparing the *pie* was to cover the top with a *crust* made of brown paper and decorate the edges according to the talents of the planners. When *serving the pie*, a large knife would be used to cut the paper, and each present would be dipped out for a good laugh.

Everyone was invited to Dr. Taylor's house to fill the candy bags on the night before the Christmas tree was to "come off." On December 21st children and adults from the fort, as well as Indians from the area, gathered for the celebration. It was quite a smash with all the children—white, black, and Indian. Carrie was the soloist, and, as she sang a hymn about the birth of Christ, some of the Indians asked Mr.

Jones, the interpreter, what the "squaw" was doing. "He told them she was invoking the great spirit to make the men's hearts better, that they might be better to the squaws, that they would help them work and make their lives easyer [sic] and happy....Quite a cute idea for Mr. J. to interpret so," wrote Marion.

As Christmas day approached, Marion longed for her family in Dallas. "I wish I was going to be home Christmas," her letter read. "You must write me just what all of you give and receive and what each of the children say and do. I hope you miss me lots."

The week before Christmas Marion had written her sister to send some Christmas cards from Dallas, admonishing her to do it quickly as mail from Dallas to Fort Sill could take as much as seven days. Besides the cards she requested for friends, she also ordered a new fan for her friend Carrie. But by Christmas Eve nothing had arrived, and Marion was dreadfully disappointed. Gifts from Dr. Taylor were delivered at the girls' house early Christmas morning, and Marion felt even worse, certain that when the cards *did* arrive the doctor would think they were an afterthought in return for the pretty riding whips he gave each young lady.

Later on Christmas day Marion and Carrie accepted an invitation from some officers to inspect the turkey-and-trimmings dinners being served to the soldiers in their quarters and at the hospital.

Caught up in the social whirl of a military post, the sophisticated young lady from Dallas wrote to her mother about Christmas at old Fort Sill in 1886:

> Dear Ma,
> Capt. Bullis took dinner with us here. He, Drs. Barbour and Kean called in the evening....
> We went to church this morning; we heard a sermon from a priest, the first time I ever saw services in a Catholic church in this country, and this is not a Catholic church.
> Mrs. Shumard says she would send her love if she ever had time but she is too busy right now.
> After dinner—The "boys" have been around to say the hop will come off Wednesday evening. So you can imagine us in our white dresses and the boys in their brass buttons and a few other garments tripping the high fantastic.
> Maybe I was a little cross about the Christmas cards, but we were so disappointed.
> Carrie gave me material for a lovely apron.
> The wind is blowing quite hard.
> Carrie and I have company for church tonight to hear the old padre, but I think I will remain en casa. The wind will nearly blow us away.
> All are well and send love.
> All except Pa write entirely too often.
> Afftly,
> M.T.B.

Adapted from Marion T. Brown: Letters From Fort Sill, 1886-1887, ed by C. Richard King, Austin, Tex.: Encino Press.

COWBOY CHRISTMAS

Major Gordon W. Lillie was known to thousands of fans of his Wild West Show as Pawnee Bill. In his younger days he had been a cowboy in the Cherokee Outlet (also known as the Cherokee Strip). According to a story he told, one of the earliest appearances of Santa Claus and a Christmas tree in that part of the Territory was in 1880 on a ranch where he worked.

Old man Constable had just returned to the Strip from running 20,000 Texas Longhorn steers to Armour and Company in Chicago. In that bustling city the cattleman had been impressed by a beautiful Christmas tree at one of the world's largest department stores. When Constable returned to the Strip, Christmas was only five days away, and he decided they had to have a tree for the ranch. When he suggested this to the other cowboys, a lively discussion ensued:

> "Whar you going to get the evergreen tree from?" asked old man Wharton.
>
> "Why, down on the Cimaroon River. It's only one day's drive from here. We'll send Scotty down in the morning."
>
> "Whar you going to get the people from to give your presents to?"
>
> "From Berry's ranch on Stillwater Creek, from Walker's ranch on Big Greasey and from Bar X horse ranch on Hell Roaring, and all the other ranches around here."
>
> "Wall, now, listen, boss. When I was a boy in Maine, I attended more than one Christmas tree celebration, and they are

run for the benefit of the kids, not the grown-up people."

> "Wall, I hadn't thought of that. I tell you what we can do. We can get that red-headed freckle-faced kid over at the Circle C ranch. He is the funniest looking kid you ever saw, and his daddy is a good fiddler. We'll have him come over to furnish the music."

Constable won out, and Scotty left the next morning to search for an evergreen along the Cimarron River down near Oklahoma country, land used at that time exclusively by large ranches in the strip for running cattle. When he found one he thought Constable would take a fancy to, he chopped the bushy cedar down, tied the branches close to the trunk, and attached it to the side of his horse. He then set off for the ranch, and when he set up the tree all the cowboys elbowed each other with delight. With great frivolity the rowdy men set about the task of stringing popcorn to decorate the tree.

Men came from all the other ranches in the area, and little Red Rankin was happier than he had been in his entire seven years. Most of his short life had been spent either on a ranch or in a covered wagon, and such *splendor* and *extravagance* was a wonder to that freckle-faced kid.

According to Lillie's account, the ranch cook served up a wild turkey dinner, which all the cowboys bragged was the best they had ever tasted. They then lit up their pipes as they sat back to enjoy the fiddle playin' of Red Rankin's pa. Pawnee Bill recalled that the boy "had just mounted his spotted hobby horse, which was the capital present presented by Dad Constable, when a volley of pistol shots rent the air, and the most unearthly cowboys' yells broke the peaceful quiet of the Christmas festivities."

Dust was flying as Ike Clubb and his friends raced up on horseback hollering that the U. S. Marshal was after them. Without bothering to dismount from their steamy horses, the riders came on into the half-dugout* serving as a ranchhouse, breaking right through the wagon sheet hung over the unfinished side of the crude structure. Breathlessly, they described how the Marshal just over the border in Caldwell, Kansas, had ordered them to forfeit their guns while in town. They had refused to obey the new law, whereupon Marshal Bill Tilghman had immediately deputized a bunch of Texas cattlemen on the spot! What a ridiculous group of emergency deputies they were—*all lit up purty well!*

Deciding there were better places for them to be, Clubb had told his cohorts as they left Caldwell, "Boys, come on. Let's not have any killing on this beautiful Christmas day. We'll go down and see Dad's Christmas tree."

Clubb and his cronies thus had turned their horses around and started to ride leisurely back to the ranch, but before they reached the Kansas border they realized that Tilghman and his men were hot on their trail. Clubb explained to Dad Constable, "So we hiked it for your ranch. They are not over half a mile behind us. They would have caught us had I not occasionally sent a Colt's bullet back over their heads, which slowed them up."

One of the cowboys suggested that Ike disguise himself in the Santa Claus suit and wig. When Tilghman arrived a few minutes later, Santa greeted him with a bottle of Old Crow and an invitation for all to join the party. Later, as the Marshal and his bunch bid Ike, Dad, and the other cowboys good-bye, "They were profuse in thanks for their entertainment and the view of the first Christmas tree ever erected in the cattle country of the Cherokee strip," recounted the great storyteller, Pawnee Bill.

*A half-dugout was a structure built into the side of a rise in the land so that half of the shelter was in the ground and half was constructed from available timber or sod.

Adapted from the *Tulsa Daily World,* December 21, 1930.

A CHRISTMAS CONFRONTATION

*"The settlers call this place the town of Stillwater."**

It was midday on Christmas Eve, 1884, when the settlers realized a confrontation with soldiers was about to take place. They left their dugout homes, which had been constructed behind their wagons and tents in the bend of the river where the banks rose in terraces, affording protection from the cold, winter weather. Leaders of the group had carefully chosen the location some three miles south of where the Arkansas City Railroad crossed Stillwater Creek. A typical dugout had one relatively good-sized and comfortable room which was dug back into the river bank's ledge; an earthen roof was propped up in the center, and a chimney was vented through the top to allow smoke to escape. Placed about 50 feet apart, these dugouts formed a quarter-circle in the bend of the creek where water and timber were abundant.

These "Boomers," as they were called, had arrived from Arkansas City by way of the Payne Trail on December 12th. They were determined to test the validity of the claims they had been making for several years under the leadership of David L. Payne that United States citizens had the

A letter written on Christmas Day, 1884, by Lieutenant M.W. Day to the Post Adjutant at Fort Reno, Indian Territory, contains this reference to Stillwater, thought to be the first recorded mention of the present city.

right to settle land in central Indian Territory not occupied by any tribe. Newspapers across the U.S. had carried fascinating stories about Payne, his Oklahoma colonists, and their repeated raids into the two million acres commonly called the Oklahoma lands (or Oklahoma country). Between 1871 and 1874, the government had surveyed the land bounded on the north by the Cherokee Outlet and on the south by the Canadian River and subdivided it into sections. As the removal of Indians from elsewhere in the United States to Indian Territory slowed, land subject to homesteading was becoming scarce elsewhere, and pressure mounted to open the Oklahoma country to *honest homeseekers*, as the Boomers were called by those sympathetic to their cause. By unsympathetic observers they were variously called intruders and raiders.

Payne and his Oklahoma Colonists waged a tremendous campaign through advertisements, circulars, and editorials promoting the homesteading of land being leased to cattle companies for grazing purposes. But Payne died suddenly in November, 1884, shortly after a momentous decision by District Judge Cassius Foster that it was not a criminal offense for citizens to settle the Oklahoma lands.

Leadership of the Boomers passed to William L. Couch, and preparations began for an immediate test of Foster's decision. They completed the 65-mile trip from Arkansas City, arriving at the pre-selected site on Stillwater Creek on December 12th. By Christmas Eve they were well settled; they organized a town company of 80 men (although more than that were present); three surveyors set about surveying lots; each family represented selected a claim; a baker opened shop; and a doctor set up practice. The population of the town exceeded 225 and included several boys and at least one woman. Lt. Day later observed, "The colonists are as a rule men of more than average intelligence and men of means." Surely they were men of determination.

Couch and the other Boomers were not surprised to see Lt. Day and about 30 members of his 9th Cavalry when they approached Stillwater on Christmas Eve. There had been clashes between Boomers and soldiers before in other parts of the territory. Lt. Day had orders to arrest the intruders, and it had taken his troop several days to travel the 20 miles from Camp Russell in bitterly cold weather. Crossing the ice-clogged Cimarron River had been extremely difficult. The soldiers had set up camp in a grove of blackjack trees near the river, hoping that the norther which had blown in would make the ice stronger for the Cavalry unit's crossing. However, the first wagon to attempt the crossing had broken through the ice near a sand bar, and the men had been forced to unload the wagon, cut the ice, and pull the wagon out with lariats. They had unloaded the second wagon in advance of crossing, removed the wheels, and attached cottonwood branches to form a sled to pull it across the ice. About 30

horses and mules had broken through the ice as they crossed the treacherous river.

Another terrible norther had blown in the Cavalry's last night on the trail, and they were cold and tired when they arrived at the Boomers' camp the day before Christmas. Nearing the village, they saw more than 200 men armed with double-barreled shotguns and Winchester rifles. The young lieutenant and his men had hoped to arrest the settlers peaceably.

Captain Couch stepped forward to say that the army had broken faith with the Boomers numerous times in the past, promising them proper trials in U.S. courts but removing them to the closest state line and releasing them without benefit of a trial that would settle the question of legality. According to Couch, prominent attorneys had advised the Boomers that they were on public domain and their arrest by the military was illegal. He said they would refuse to surrender to anything but civil process, and he vowed that he and his followers would defend themselves with guns if necessary.

Day's letter to his commanding officer later that day described the confrontation: "Though I had 30 men on a skirmish line, as they were densely massed I hesitated to give the command to fire as the slaughter would have been great. I have done all I can to make the arrest without resort to arms, and would therefore request to be informed if I am to treat this body of men as insurgents, and after calling on them to give up their arms and submit to arrest, to open fire on them."

Couch's account of this affair was slightly different: "We were ordered to surrender at once, declaring he [Day] would open fire on us if we refused. I asked by what authority he ordered us to surrender, to which he replied: 'Military authority.' He said he didn't propose to discuss the matter but would form his line and give us five minutes to surrender or be shot down. We said we would return the fire. He then detailed five men to seize and tie me, but as the detail advanced we halted them, and after I made a little speech, he ordered his men back into line and ordered them to fire. Seeing we were determined to protect ourselves, he made the excuse that his men were freezing to death there, and that he would go to camp and allow us until morning [Christmas] to make up our minds.''

They were convinced they were not hurting anyone except cattlemen, who already had spent thousands of dollars trying to keep them out.

Mentioned in Day's report was one woman, Josiphene [sic] Allen, who with her husband and two children had moved all their household furniture to their crude new home at Stillwater. According to several accounts, this plucky little woman refused the Cavalry's offer of protection, responding that she felt safer with her Boomer friends. Turning to her husband with a revolver in her hand, she exclaimed, "Take that, Allen, and stand by the boomers!" Her remark spread rapidly through the camp and boosted the morale of the men. It became the spirit call of the Boomers.

The articulate William Couch convinced Day to allow them to telegraph the President of the United States for a swift ruling. Young Lt. Day used the delay to contact his superior officer for instructions on handling the intruders, knowing arrest of the entire settlement would require reinforcements.

The rest of Christmas Eve and for many days following, arms were laid down, and the two factions relaxed while strategy and communications were prepared. Christmas day was not spent at church or with Christmas tree celebrations for the 9th Cavalry or the Stillwater Boomers; Couch and his people spent Christmas day formulating a telegram to President Chester A. Arthur, and Day spent the morning writing an account of the events of Christmas Eve. "I have 39 men," he concluded. "I have five days forage and rations, but will send one wagon with five men for one week's rations and forage. There is an abundance of wood, water and grazing in this vicinity."

Couch's message to the President demonstrated both his determination and his intelligence:

> His Excellency, Chester A. Arthur
> President of the United States,
>   Washington D.C.
> Regarding the fact of a large number of law abiding citizens now residing upon the Oklahoma lands, who have exhausted every expedient that human ingenuity could invent to have the title of these lands settled that we are upon, are peaceable law abiding settlers disturbing no one and violating no law of the United States, that we are now confronted by a detachment of U.S. troops who demand our surrender threatening to fire upon us if we do not quietly sub-

mit to an arrest which would result in our again being dragged to some State line to be turned loose without recourse to law. We are unwilling to submit to military arrest while under the jurisdiction of civil law. Do you assume responsibility to declare us insurgent citizens of the United States, who are located upon and occupying the public domain, holding as we do that Section 2147R[evised]S[tatutes] does not apply to this land as it is not Indian country? The title being in the United States we pray your excellency to order a stay in the action of the troops pending your action in this matter. An early consideration and reply will be gratefully accepted by thousands of honest homeseekers throughout the United States. Reply to Arkansas City, Kansas.

Obdtly yours, W.L. Couch

The weather was cold and wet on Christmas day, and the soldiers remained in camp without tents. Several men were on sick report with frostbite, and one man was threatened with pneumonia. Relations between the settlers and soldiers gradually would relax, and the Stillwater doctor treated the sick soldier before he was sent back to Camp Russell. The Boomers even loaned Lt. Day a spring wagon and team to go out and meet the ration wagon when it arrived a few days later.

In the warmth of their dugout homes the patient homesteaders waited. Perhaps some read the Christmas story in their Bibles, while others contemplated the numerous attempts at settlement already made and the long days ahead that they must wait before the bitter rivalry for land between colonists and cattlemen would be resolved.

"Let the people understand this thing," stated a *Chicago Tribune* editorial a month later. "The question is not between Indians and the whites....It is simply and solely between rich cattle trespassers and poor settlers." On January 31 they were escorted back across the state line into Kansas.

Lt. M.W. Day was subsequently reprimanded for "being on terms entirely too familiar with the intruders." He was cautioned in this respect and informed that "the performance of duty should not be embarrassed by exhibition of sympathy for the boomers." His superiors became so incensed over his relationship with the settlers that he was relieved of his command at Camp Russell on February 6, 1885.

Four years later the question of the Oklahoma lands was finally decided. Individual settlement became a reality with the great Land Run of April 22, 1889. William L. Couch, many members of his family, and other Boomers who had spent a lonely and cold Christmas by Stillwater Creek eventually realized their dream. Four years later they joined the rush to stake their claims on land they had worked for 11 years to call their own.

PERMANENT SETTLERS CELEBRATE

CHRISTMAS LIKE "BACK IN THE STATES"

The first Christmas tree in Sayre (then called Riverton), O. T., was held on December 25, 1901, at the Convention Hall. Decorations were mostly homemade, and the tree (barely visible in the background) was made of mesquite bushes nailed together with each twig wrapped in cotton batting. The hall was lit by kerosene lamps with tin reflectors. (Photo courtesy Western History Collections, University of Oklahoma Library.)

As the territorial land opened to permanent settlement in stages, beginning with the Land Run of April 22, 1889, into the Unassigned Lands of central Oklahoma, frontier towns sprang up like prairie flowers. Trains, wagons, and horses brought an influx of people with the family and religious customs of various regions of the United States, as well as many foreign countries. As communities formed, neighbors turned to one another, especially at holiday time when the yearnings for friends and loved ones *back in the States* and across the ocean became the greatest.

Holidays were community events as much as family occasions, especially in rural localities where folks who had staked a full 160-acre quarter-section were relatively isolated. Holidays were a joyous time for children to play, teenagers to experience the first pangs of love, young mothers to compare recipes and remedies, men to discuss crops and politics, and grandparents to reminisce about Christmases past.

In those early years of settlement, Christmas was celebrated by *having or giving a Christmas tree* in a community building: a church, school, or perhaps a commercial building. Committees were assigned duties several weeks in advance to locate and chop the tree, decorate it, and plan the program preceding the presentation of gifts by Santa Claus.

Selection of a tree depended upon what part of O.T. or I.T. they were in. Oklahoma offered as wide a variety of Christmas trees as there were different terrains in this varied land of hills and prairies. On the roll-ing plains of the central portion of the territory, native evergreens were scarce, so blackjacks or other native oak trees were used. On occasion, hardy men and boys would go for miles to find a native red cedar. To the east, in the hilly and wooded sections of Indian Territory, there was an abundance of trees for use at Christmas, even the traditional pine.

At Boggy Depot, Indian Territory, in the Choctaw Nation, the young people of the community decorated the school building with cedar branches gathered from the woods near the Kiamichi Mountains. All the families brought their presents to be distributed at the one big community Christmas tree. Afterwards the men all went to the blacksmith shop, where they had a high old time shooting off charges of gunpowder using two blacksmith's anvils. Women and children were excluded from these festivities on the pretext they might get hurt. Perhaps other things went on which the women and children needed protection from, like a swig or two from a jug and an occasional shady story. These details have not been preserved.

There had been no killing frost by Christmas of 1889, as remembered by Mrs. Edith B. Russell, so the windows and doors of their home were left open when friends joined them for Christmas dinner. Everyone loved the Christmas tree her dad had fashioned from a blackjack tree. The children of the family had spent many hours stringing popcorn, which he draped on the branches. He wrapped each branch and twig of the tree with cotton to look like snow, although the weather outside was very mild. Throughout the fall her father had saved the tinfoil separating the layers of his plug tobacco, and from this he carefully cut out icicles to add sparkle to the limbs of the blackjack Christmas tree.

In the frontier town of Edmond, the first Christmas tree was celebrated in the school house, which also served as the place of worship for all denominations during the first months following the April '89 Run. Mrs. George Brauer remembered that here, too, a large blackjack tree replaced the traditional evergreen as the centerpiece for an evening of recitations, songs, and dancing of the popular square dance, waltz, and schottische.

At 9:00 o'clock on Christmas Eve, all the families of Hennessey poured into the new Smith Building to await the arrival of Santa Claus. As in programs all over the territories, Santa was the center of attention. He usually wore a homemade red suit and whiskers made of cotton and was played by a jolly citizen clever enough to keep up a humorous commentary for the enjoyment of the adults while bringing joy and wonder to the young children. He presented little bags of candy, frequently an apple or orange, and gifts, often placed directly on the branches of the tree. There were special gifts for poor children of the community who might receive nothing at home on Christmas morning. One Christmas Eve in the little town of Randlett, much excitement erupted when Santa's cotton whiskers caught fire.

By necessity, towns made frequent use of any building large enough to hold a crowd. In Yukon it was the Valley View School where the celebration took place. The decoration committee had popped a 50-pound larder of popcorn for stringing and making popcorn balls. Timber was scarce at Elk City, and no church or school had been constructed by December of 1898, so the neighbors gathered in a dugout on Christmas Eve. Little Sarah Addie Wheeler went to her first Christmas tree in that dugout and never forgot the Christmas spirit they all felt. Perhaps the dugout carved into the side of a slope was not unlike the manger she had heard about in the Bible.

A small dugout also was used for church at Cordell, where the men built a brush arbor and hung lanterns for the Christmas tree celebration. Twelve miles south of Sulphur, at Oil Creek, the church building was so small that when the tree was erected in 1886 there was no room left for the people. A log heap fire was built, and all the families stood outside by the fire while presents were delivered.

One-room churches, school houses, dugouts, commercial buildings—even the new storeroom of a local Blackwell businessman—became holiday gathering places. The first Christmas in Blackwell following the opening of the Cherokee Outlet in September of 1893 was documented in a scrapbook by Mrs. Celeste Ball May. "The first Christmas for Blackwell has come and gone," she wrote, "and our town has renewed cause for congratulations in the manner it was celebrated."

The minister of the church and members of the Sunday School classes presented a devotional program on Christmas Eve as the first part of the two-night celebration. On Christmas night, music, recitation, and drama comprised the special

This snowy scene of south Bartlesville was taken at Christmas, 1892, and is the oldest known photograph of the city of Bartlesville. (Photo courtesy History Room, Bartlesville Public Library.)

Christmas treat. "The building where both entertainments were held was a frame store," said Mrs. May. "Carpenters worked all day Sunday to get in the windows and did not succeed in hanging the door."

This did not matter because the weather was mild, and the people stood in the street to watch the performance. Into the bare building folks had brought all sorts of furnishings from their homes to make the structure more homey: pictures, portieres*, rugs, lamps, and tissue paper flowers. They hoped to make it like Christmas "back home."

The drama began with a march, according to Mrs. May, "led by Uncle Jon-athan and Aunt Columbia in costume followed by children representing the different sections of the country..., sunny south with palm leaf fan to the frozen, fur-clad north."

The stage backdrop was an *"old-fash-ioined fireplace"* created from brick-col-ored building paper marked with chalk and hung with stockings. In front of this setting children on the stage pretended to sleep while waiting for Santa to appear. All feigned sleep well except a little black boy who delighted the audience with his impatient antics, peeking up the chim-ney for Santa. When he finally arrived, Santa wore a fur outfit and flowing beard.

The children were so thrilled and excited that the two youngest little girls, age four, backed off the stage in fright. Although not part of the program, this caused much merriment, and fortunately the girls were not hurt.

In retrospect, Mrs. May thought all this merriment helped the pioneers overcome homesick feelings which might have overshadowed them on that first Christmas in Oklahoma Territory. Although the 1893 program in Blackwell was typical of those taking place in many frontier communities, it is interesting to note that no tree was mentioned in Mrs. May's account. A fireplace served as the focal point of the entertainment.

By 1893 numerous churches were well-established in El Reno, which took its name from nearby Fort Reno (an army post established in 1875). Although the Christmas tree was favored in most churches, there were variations from that tradition. At the local Baptist Church, Santa descended a chimney, then tore it down and distributed the parts to his little friends. A *Bridge Entertainment* took weeks of planning by members of the Methodist Episcopal Church South. Men handy with hammers and nails constructed a bridge inside the church with a Christmas tree placed at each end. A group of children was selected to play the role of brownies, or elves, and the drama was carefully rehearsed. On Christmas Eve all members of the church gathered to see the elaborate program. As the brownies crossed the bridge, Santa appeared from underneath, and the brownies peppered him with snowballs. The performance was accompanied by a *realistic snowstorm*.

Those first Christmases in territorial towns were mixed with feelings of expectation, joy, and gratitude for the new life open to them, and simultaneously many felt fear, disappointment, and loneliness for loved ones left behind. By re-creating the customs of Christmas out here in Oklahoma country, they could feel the spirit of the season just as they had *back in the States*.

*Portieres were curtains hung in a doorway.

HOLIDAY GIFTS AND GEWGAWS

Gifts have always been an important part of the joy of Christmas, and the years before statehood were no exception. Even the smallest frontier towns had drug stores well stocked with gift items: dolls, toys, and *all sorts of gewgaws* for holiday decorations. Many larger towns in Oklahoma Territory were located on major railroad lines, and in young cities like Guthrie and Oklahoma City the assortment of merchandise and food available sometimes is surprising to those who assume all Oklahoma pioneers led a primitive and spartan existence. Many people from rural areas shopped in these cities when their towns did not have the products they desired. Grocery markets, even in the years before statehood stocked wide varieties of food, including fancy canned goods, fresh produce, and dried fruits. Confections and baked goods were plentiful in most frontier cities.

The *Kingfisher Free Press* ran an ad in December of 1890 offering numerous suggestions for the Christmas shopper. One headline stated, "Do You Know That Christmas Is Coming? Come In and Visit Our Store While In The City." That store stocked many fine items: an alligator skin purse, a bill book, and a nice ink stand were offered for father; for mother a Bible, a Haviland sugar and creamer, and a Limoges plate were suggested; for the baby of the family there were rag dolls, rubber balls, telephone chimes, and woolly dogs; for a friend the store had a book of poems or a writing desk; grandmothers might like a spectacle case or a work box; and grandfathers might need a reading glass, a shaving mug, or a diary. For a little boy there were mechanical toys, a tool chest, and unbreakable iron toys; for litle girls the store had a doll bed and dresser, a *really and truly range*, and a kettle and stew pan. For the *best girl* (known today as a girlfriend), the management suggested a glove or handkerchief box, a bottle of perfume, or a box of fine candies. A young lady might give her *best fellow* a traveling case in leather or ebony or a cuff and collar box.

Some historians have concluded that gifts like these seemed useless to people who needed the bare essentials of life, but there is vast documentation of the *relative* prosperity of many settlers. They desired—and could afford—some of the nicer things of life as well as the necessities. Ella Martin McKowen, who was an 89er, recalled many years later that on her first Christmas in Oklahoma City in 1889, her long, black, ribbed stocking had a funny bulge from the copy of *Swiss Family Robinson* left in it by Santa Claus.

Life in the cities, almost from their founding, had a surprising degree of sophistication and an active social life. Lawyers, bankers, businessmen, and individuals from all classes saw in this beautiful land an opportunity for success. Ready access to railroads—the same ones which had brought many of them here and had determined the locations of principal towns—insured that settlers did not have to forfeit all the comforts they had enjoyed *back in the States*. There certainly were instances of hardship and a period of adjustment, especially for those coming from foreign lands; they had to contend with language and cultural barriers. But these problems were not as all-encompassing in Oklahoma Territory as is sometimes assumed.

Homesickness generated intense feeling during those first Christmases in Indian and Oklahoma Territories. Mrs. Tom B. Ferguson received a very special gift from Santa Claus at Christmas in 1889, as she recalled many years later. This gift dispelled the Christmas blues on her first Christmas away from her loved ones.

She and her husband had come to Watonga from Kansas to set up a weekly newspaper. The funny little town was full of strange people, according to Mrs. Ferguson, and she described the town as "a mudhole in the middle of the street with seven saloons." Although she knew it took courage to *go pioneering*, she could not help feeling blue as she told Christmas stories to her two very young sons on Christmas morning. One of the children was old enough to expect a visit from Santa Claus, but chances seemed slim for that to occur.

Wondering what she would prepare for Christmas dinner and feeling very sorry for herself, she heard a firm knock at the door. Opening it to the unexpected visitor, Mrs. Ferguson thought her tale to the children of Santa had become a reality; there stood a genuine Santa, the German baker from across the street. Over his arm was a basket filled with delicacies. The robust man wore a fur cap which came down almost to his thick, gray side whiskers, and his friendly face resembled the ruddy countenance of picturebook Santas. She had difficulty understanding his thick accent, but she comprehended the meaning of his reference to strangers in a strange land as he set the straw basket down and patted one of her boys on the head.

After the friendly neighbor returned to his bakeshop, the young mother knew that things would be all right for her family in this new land. "The Christmas spirit remained, the tears and blue atmosphere had disappeared as if by magic," recalled the grateful pioneer woman. "The basket, when unpacked, revealed many treasures for small boys and first aids for Christmas dinner. But best of all, it was the genuine cheer of having been remembered that made the day a happy one."

Portions from "Oklahoma, the Beautiful Land," by the 1889ers.

A SECONDHAND GIFT

Although attractive selections of merchandise were readily available, many individuals liked to use their imaginations in gift-giving just as they do now. A girl in Shawnee thought of a unique method of Christmas shopping in 1907. For five years she had kept all sorts of gifts received on various occasions, including party favors and prizes. Taking care that all the items were fresh and new-looking, she selected gifts from her own *store*. Not wishing to deceive the recipients, she composed a poem to accompany each gift:

At Christmastime in years gone by
Friends have been good to me-
So what they gave so freely then
I'll pass along to thee.

Treasure the gift and keep it fresh
Till Christmas next year, when
You'll find it quite convenient, friend
To pass it on again.

So push a good thing right along-
'Twill help some worthy neighbor
It's handy when you're short of cash
And saves a lot of labor!

FRONTIER CITY—1907

Instant cities of 10,000-plus sprang up at Guthrie and Oklahoma City with the Run of 1889. During the next 18 years prior to statehood, life became quite sophisticated in these frontier cities. On November 16, 1907, the Twin Territories joined to form the state of Oklahoma with a mock wedding between a settler, representing "Mr. Oklahoma Territory," and an Indian maiden, depicting "Miss Indian Territory." The "marriage" took place at Guthrie, the Territorial capital, as part of elaborate statehood day events.

The following month Oklahomans celebrated their first Christmas as a state, the 46th star. Despite financial stringency nationally, owing to the Panic of 1907, merchants in Oklahoma City claimed that Christmas sales that year were the most lucrative ever, breaking all records for holiday merchandising. Trains full of shoppers arrived daily from nearby towns, and businessmen hired extra salespeople and extended shopping hours into the evening. Local restauranteur Mr. Reub, owner of Reub's Cafe at 111 North Broadway, remarked to a friend, "The busy crowds will stop to eat. We're making every effort to feed the crowds. We can always tell when the trains arrive by the rush at our tables."

Mr. Houghton realized the results of a promotional trip to El Reno earlier in the month. He purposefully attended the big ball given for soldiers being discharged at Fort Reno. An astute businessman, he used the opportunity to promote his Christmas merchandise, and his efforts resulted in business beyond anything expected.

Shoppers crowded into a new bookstore on West Main to peruse the extensive selection of hundreds of new volumes, including *Read's Modern Eloquence*, numerous dictionaries, encyclopedias, and histories.

Longtime merchants of men's and boys' clothing, Gerson Brothers' Store was having the greatest business in its history. A major competitor, Bloch Brothers', declared a pre-holiday sale, and people jammed the store clear to the rear doors to take advantage of the bargains. The Blochs' expectation of a clean sweep of their holiday line certainly came true.

The entire work force at Parrott and Durland Confectioners worked frantically in the store, bakery, and candy factory to fill orders for cream, cakes, and candy. At 211 West Main, their rival, Mr. Doerr, joined his workmen in the factory room where they were "making stick candy faster than it was possible to count."

With retail and wholesale business booming, Doerr took a moment to reminisce about earlier days in the young city: "Seventeen years ago [1890] I was selling candy on the street corner in Oklahoma City. My business at that time consisted of a cart and a few pounds of candy, but today we manufacture all grades of candy, from the cheapest stick to the finest chocolates and bon-bons."

31

Merchants of all kinds were busy just before Christmas, 1907, in Oklahoma City. Mr. Westfall, who operated a drug company, guaranteed Christmas morning delivery of boxes of candy. Mr. Downey, of Downey and Thomas Furniture Company, was shipping an unexpected amount of furniture to nearby towns in every direction in time for the holidays. F. W. Miller's trunk company offered all manner of leather trunks, hand bags, and small leather novelties like purses, music rolls, and comb and brush sets, all popular Christmas items.

While in town, many shoppers stopped at the Yale nickelodeons (forerunner of today's movie theaters), advertised as two of the largest in the city. Boasting both amusing and educational shows, comic ones were interspersed with travelogues about China and Japan. On alternate days, the management included illustrated songs for sing-along and encouraged all to attend with claims that "We cater only to the best people, and at all times maintain the best of order." (Apparently this was not always true of nickelodeons, which were named for the price of admission, five cents.)

Social life in cities like Guthrie and Oklahoma City thrived on the Christmas activities of many new organizations and clubs: the 46th Star Club (named for statehood), the Philomathea Study Club, Kosmos Club, and the Chafing Dish Club. The latter group, perhaps the most exclusive in Oklahoma City, accepted only members of the highest social order for the afternoon club. On Monday preceding Christmas in 1907, members met at Mrs. Henry Overholser's beautiful new home on the northern edge of town on Northwest 15th Street. No doubt, much of the ladies' conversation centered around the New Year's Day breakfast to be held there. Four hundred invitations had been mailed, and the party was sure to be quite elegant.

The Overholser Opera House, built by Mrs. Overholser's husband, offered a special bill of professional dramatic performances by touring companies during Christmas week. "District Leader" was described as a musical with reason, and another musical, "Isle of Spice," featured 20 whistling song hits and unique dances. A group of musical troubadours called "Black Patti" also performed. Taking guests to a matinee or an evening performance at the Overholser was a popular holiday recreation of that era.

As in earlier days, churches played central roles in Christmas celebrations. By 1907, however, fashions were changing, and some churches dispensed with Christmas trees, substituting more *fashionable* decorations such as fans and umbrellas. St. Luke's Methodist Episcopal Church used a gigantic umbrella to support presents for the children of the church. A Christmas tree was given at St. Paul's Episcopal Church with presents for various missions in town.

Provision was made for *the pleasure and comfort of the poor and other unfortunates,* including inmates of the county poor farm and city and county jails. Under-Sheriff Harvey Garrison planned a dinner of turkey, cranberry sauce, pie, and potatoes for his charges at the county jail,

For little Henry Ione's first Christmas—1906—her parents, Mr. and Mrs. Henry Overholser, invited 100 guests to view the large electrically lighted Christmas tree in the parlor of their elegant home on the corner of Hudson and N.W. 15th Street. (Photo courtesy Overholser Mansion, Oklahoma Historical Society.)

but city authorities made no plans for *Christmas edibles* in the city jail as they did not expect anyone to be incarcerated by the city that day. However, a spokesman for the city assured the public that "In case some malefactor is detained, a special dinner will be provided."

Salvation Army members on down-town Oklahoma City street corners collected money from charitable citizens passing their collection pots. The money enabled the Salvation Army to deliver more than 200 dinners to the poor. On Christmas Eve workers transformed the army hall with decorations and a Christmas tree to "gladden the hearts of children whose punctured stockings might otherwise be unnoticed by the Good Saint Nick.''

Perhaps churches of the cities and towns were abandoning the custom of the Christmas tree because of the increased availability of trees to families for their homes. Even household decorations had become more elaborate. Mr. and Mrs. J.W. Pryor entertained their children and a few little friends in 1907 with a tree strung with tiny vari-colored electric bulbs, forsaking the traditional but dangerous candles of years past. The tree was surmounted by a large crimson bell and encircled by garlands of smaller bells.

Pine and cedar trees, along with other *necessary adjuncts to the old-fashioned Christmas*, were shipped or hauled to Oklahoma City from all parts of the new state. Red-berried holly came from the cross-timber section of Texas, and pine shrubs came from the piney hills near the Oklahoma-Arkansas border. A large supply of trees came from the north and south forks of the Canadian River, from the Arbuckle Mountains of south-central Oklahoma, and from the hills of the eastern section of the state. Farmers in Oklahoma County hauled red cedar trees into town from the surrounding countryside and sold them on street corners, along with sprigs of mistletoe* knocked from branches of trees along rural creeklines, where it thrived.

It was still a popular Victorian custom among some families to mount a small tree on a round parlor table, where candles and decorations were out of reach of curious toddlers.

Christmas feasts the year of statehood promised to be sumptuous with *an exceedingly plentiful outlay of toothsome and tempting delicacies*. Grocers advertised strawberries for 50 cents a box (an astounding price for those days), Malaga grapes, oranges, apples, lettuce, tomatoes, and radishes. Fatted ducks were marked to sell at 17 cents a pound; dressed geese at 15 cents, and turkeys at 15 cents. Fresh cranberries could be purchased for 10 cents and 15 cents a quart.

Thus this brand new state, the 46th star, born of the union of Oklahoma and Indian Territories, began its climb to prosperity and prominence as one of the last frontiers. Pioneers who considered themselves modern and progressive had led the way. In the span of one man's lifetime, the holiday customs of this new land—with its Christmas trees, Santa Clauses, and holiday foods—have not really changed very much. Songs are still sung in churches on Christmas Eve, busy merchants offer pre-holiday sales, the Salvation Army cares for the downtrodden, and traditional foods warm the soul as families and friends gather at Christmas time in a more mature frontier, Oklahoma of 1982.

Mistletoe, an ancient holiday symbol, was found in abundance in this young state and was named the state flower, although it is a parasite and not a flower at all.

PART II

MEMORIES AND TRADITIONS

MEMORIES OF CHRISTMASES
AFTER STATEHOOD

A DOLL NAMED BYRNIE

As the train pulled away from the Oklahoma City depot, five-year-old Mary Elizabeth Edwards pressed her nose against the cold glass on that December morning of 1912. She watched the depot disappear as the train headed south for Texas. It was nearing Christmas, and Mr. and Mrs. R.J. Edwards were taking their five young children on their annual journey to Monroe, Louisiana, to spend the holiday with Mrs. Edwards' father, John S. Handy, and the rest of her family. Mary Elizabeth Thach still recalls the hard-backed seats in the depots at Fort Worth and Shreveport during long waits between transferring trains before they arrived at the river town of Monroe.

It had been several weeks since her fifth birthday on November 16, and Mary Elizabeth was too young to realize her birthday coincided with another important birthday—Oklahoma's statehood. When bells rang, horns honked, and people shouted on November 16, 1907, to celebrate the union of Oklahoma and Indian Territories as the 46th state, Mary Elizabeth Edwards had been born, the fourth child and first daughter of Sadie H. and R.J. Edwards. Her father, founder of one of the first municipal bond companies in

the United States, was away from home that day; he was in Chicago helping Oklahoma banks avert a financial crisis during the short Panic of 1907.

Christmas of 1912 was especially memorable for Mary Elizabeth. Grandfather Handy had sent several workers from his wholesale grocery company in Monroe out to the forest where they had cut down a huge wild holly tree. They had placed it in the big hall of the Handy house on River Front Street, and, when the family gathered for gift giving, Mary Elizabeth would get her first glimpse of the favorite gift of her entire childhood, a Stockinet girl doll and a Schoenhut boy doll sitting on an elaborate doll steamer trunk. She never would forget that moment. Her father smiled at his daughter's delight at the dolls he had purchased at Marshall Field in Chicago. She promptly named the girl doll "Byrnie" and the boy doll "Bradley" because on Christmas night she would be the flower girl in the wedding of her Aunt Byrnie and her fiance, Bradley.

Throughout the holiday season in Monroe the children loved to watch fireworks being shot along the river behind the big houses on the main street of town.

The little girl reaching for her new doll was born the day Oklahoma became a state, November 16, 1907. Mary Elizabeth Thach of Oklahoma City still has one of the two dolls she received this Christmas of 1912 at her grandfather's home in Louisiana, where the Christmas tree was a wild holly. She and her brothers, Archie (in football uniform), Beverly (baby), and John (hidden behind his mother's arms), all still live in Oklahoma City.   (Photo courtesy Mrs. W. Thomas Thach.)

The Handy family had an ample supply since the wholesale grocery company also handled the sale of fireworks.

The train trip home was not such a pleasant memory because Mrs. Edwards insisted on using the new doll trunk to transport fresh oranges back to Oklahoma City from her father's wholesale house. Oranges were rare and far more important to Mother than to a five-year-old girl who thought her new doll clothes deserved their rightful container!

After Grandfather Handy died in 1914, Christmases were celebrated in Oklahoma City with the tree held early on Christmas Eve in the Edwards' home. As soon as baby sister Sadie, born in 1916, was old enough to stand straight and still, she was outfitted with an angel robe made of cheesecloth. Her older brother Archie fashioned angel wings from coat hanger wire and crepe paper. With halo slightly askew, the little angel posed beside the family Christmas tree, the soft glow of live candles reflecting on her dimpled cheeks. Little Sadie was lovingly called "Angel Child" by her parents.

Winters were cold and windy in those days, and little girls wore long underwear and black cotton stockings. Of course, these stockings were perfect to hang for Santa because they were quite long and stretched even longer when filled with candy and fruit on Christmas Eve. Those warm underclothes felt especially good to Mary Elizabeth as the Edwards family walked the seven blocks to St. Paul's Episcopal Cathedral late on Christmas Eve after gifts had been exchanged and the children had received their toys. She still can hear the crunching of snow underfoot and smell the huge pine trees on the corner by Dr. Garrison's house as Mother and Father Edwards took their six children to the midnight service. The beautiful church was bedecked with smilax all around the arch and capitols.

Even after Mary Elizabeth married W. Thomas Thach and had children of her own, she treasured the Christmas doll Byrnie she had received when she was five. (Bradley got lost or was broken sometime over the years.) The steamer trunk filled with doll clothes and the stocking doll named for her aunt are still among Mrs. Thach's prized possessions as she and Oklahoma celebrate the diamond anniversary of their simultaneous births.

A DOUBLE CHRISTMAS WEDDING

For many 89ers, gifts were available but money wasn't! W.N. Shumate, the late retired policeman, recalled one of the first Christmases he had after making the Run of 1889. On a 160-acre tract near Taloga, Billy was herding cattle by the time he was 14, and he knew the work well. One Christmas, when he was raising his own cattle and crops and also serving as justice of the peace in his spare time, cash was definitely lacking.

"It was Christmas Eve," he recalled in later years, "and I didn't have one cent with which to buy my wife, Laura, a gift, and I was feeling mighty low."

Just when he was ready to go home, here came four young people wanting him to marry them. Like a gift from heaven, the fee they paid for his services as justice of the peace would give him Christmas money.

"I made a double wedding out of that

in no time flat! That's the best Christmas I have had yet," he recounted in 1947. "I was able to make my wife's holiday happier when I didn't think there would be any Christmas for her at all."

Adapted from the Oklahoma City Times, December 25, 1947.

THE DOLL AT THE TOP OF THE TREE

Early in the summer of 1906, seven-year-old Edna Mae McCracken of Perry, Oklahoma Territory, and her cousins were playing with her china doll when several boys dashed up, grabbed the doll, and ran. As they fled from the outraged little girls, the doll dropped and was smashed beyond repair.

No stores sold dolls at that time of year, but her papa and mama, Thomas and Jennie McCracken, promised a tearful Edna a new doll by Christmas, a long wait for a little girl.

McCracken had made the run on horseback into the Cherokee Strip in 1893 and was now a salesman for the Baker Company, traveling from town to town in a horse and buggy. He always brought a gift to Edna when he came home, and he tried repeatedly to buy the longed-for doll, but none was available even in larger towns.

When Christmas finally came, the McCrackens joined their neighbors at the Baptist Church Christmas Eve program, where there was a large native cedar tree and treats of oranges, apples, nuts, and candy. Some parents brought special gifts to be placed on or under the tree. When Edna walked into the church, her eyes were instantly drawn to the top of the tree. Hanging on a high branch was a beautiful German bisque doll with long, brown curly hair and blown glass eyes. She was dressed in pink silk and wore a fancy bonnet. "There's my doll! There's my doll!" she told her parents.

It was an endless wait until the end of the program, but finally they began calling out names and handing out gifts. All of the gifts had been dispersed except the lovely china doll. Then Edna's name was called! She raced to the front to claim her precious prize. Edna loved the doll all her life.

"Edna passed away in 1969 at age 71, but her doll is still loved," recalls Glynn Munger Cochran of Castle. "She was my mother and gave me her doll."

"I recall one year—about 1933—my daddy, Mr. William A. Munger, of Perry, took some of us children out into the country for a tree. All he could find was a small blackjack that still had its leaves," says Mrs. Cochran. "Talk about being disappointed—we were. But Mother dusted the leaves, set it on a stand, and we decorated the ol' brown thing. When the lights were turned on, each leaf shone like it had been waxed, and it was very pretty! Of all the trees we've ever had through the years, it was my favorite."

FIRST COMMUNITY CHRISTMAS TREE
AT MARSHALL OKLA. 1816

This 1916 street scene at Marshall, Oklahoma (founded in 1890), represents one of the earliest examples of outdoor Christmas decorations by a town in Oklahoma. The tree is so large that people are standing underneath it, and the sign over it reads, "Welcome." (Photo courtesy Helen F. Holmes, Guthrie.)

A CHRISTMAS BABY

Over the years there has been a lot of conversation in the Ruth family about Christmas of 1916. According to a long-standing tradition the folks *did the tree* after the children went to bed on Christmas Eve so it was sparklingly new on Christmas morning. That custom was altered in 1916 because of the impending arrival of a new baby. Everything was done well in advance, and on Christmas Day little Kent Ruth made his first appearance. To this day he claims that his older

41

sister Helen "remembers and complains loudly to all who will listen of the Christmas I ruined for her because I was thoughtless enough to arrive on Christmas Day itself."

Catty-corner across the street from the Ruth home was the Mennonite Church, which had been the first organized in Geary by German settlers in 1897. The following year it had been moved from its original location three miles north of town to its present site and enlarged to accommodate the growing community.

This was the scene of many memorable Christmases for the three Ruth children as they were growing up across the street. Until recent years a program was always presented by the children of the church on Christmas Eve. Kent Ruth, now a well-known Oklahoma author, recalls that everyone had to recite *a piece*, even if it was only a line or two: "My big worry was forgetting my lines and having my big brother, Nelson, on the back row wiggle his ears at me." Helen remembers when the native cedar tree was still lit with candles. Older boys in the church stood near the tree with mops and a bucket of water in case a fire erupted.

At the conclusion of the program the children were rewarded with treats, usually a grocery sack filled with goodies: multi-colored twists, peanut clusters, candy corn, XXX mints, nuts, and an apple and orange. Kent's feelings of fear are still vivid; as the sacks were distributed alphabetically by the Sunday School superintendent, "Amstutz, Base, Dalke, Krehbiel, Leck, Lehman, Ringleman.... How I'd worry that they'd run out of sacks before getting to Ruth! Beyond, of course, there were plenty of Warkentins and Zweiachers..., but they could do their own worrying!"

CHINABERRIES, TOO!

In the little town of Loveall, the community Christmas tree was much like those in other parts of central Oklahoma with a pot-luck supper, program, and Santa in a homemade suit. Mildred Kessler recalls that besides popcorn and red berries decorating the native cedar tree, chinaberries also were used. Their delicate, glassy quality added sparkle to the huge tree laden with dolls and toys (brought by loving parents) for Santa to present to the little ones.

DOUGH-FACE

The little house near Wayne, I.T., was filled with laughing children and young parents on Christmas Eve of 1907. One young mother was not sure how the children would react to the trick her husband was planning to play on them. Mr. Berry had asked her to make up some dough, roll it thin, and spread it over his face. She had never heard of a *dough-face* before, but he thought it would make a funny surprise. With the dough covering his head and face, she punched out eyes and a nose. He then put on his hat and pulled his coat up around his neck. A cap pistol completed his props for the masquerade.

Mrs. Berry went back inside, and soon he approached the cabin ringing a bell. The children didn't know what to think. Leslie exclaimed, "Santa Claus, please don't shoot me," recounted Mrs. Berry years later. "Leroy was scared and started to run through the window, and if Mr. Berry had not caught him in time he would have." With the masquerader revealed, all was joyful again, and the family had its Christmas tree.

Adapted from Chronicles of Oklahoma, "Grandma Berry's Ninety Years in Oklahoma," by Becky Berry, XLV (1967).

THE SWEET FRAGRANCE OF ORANGES

As a child growing up in the country in the 1920s, Lillian Russell's memories of Christmas approaching are very precious to her. The family lived outside Depew, a small oil boom town.

"I could tell that Christmas was not far off because Mother would bring out the beautiful blue glass bowl with the fluted edges from the glass china cabinet," recalls Lillian. "Then she would fill it with oranges. The smell of oranges permeated the air, and I associated that aroma with the coming of Santa Claus because that was the only time we had oranges dis-

played in the blue bowl in the middle of the big, round dining table.

"There were signs of Christmas all around. Mother would start baking days in advance and carefully place the pies and cakes in the well-house to keep cool. She never baked less than six to eight pies at one time and several cakes. The one thing she made that will vividly remain in my memory was the Lady Baltimore cake. She won prizes at the fair with her baking, and this would have taken top honors. There were at least five layers of marvelous white cake, and between each layer was a cream filling with nuts, coconut, and sometimes dates. The top and sides were covered with white boiled frosting and then covered with cups of freshly grated coconut. The cake stood nearly a foot high when finished and was placed on a freshly ironed, hand-embroidered table cloth on a special table we children could reach.

"Those were the 'good old days' before we were aware of words like *diet* and *calories*. Those were the days when we had real butter and cream so thick we had to cut it with a knife," the city resident now remembers. "We made our own bread, cheese, jellies, and canned goods. For Christmas dinner we found our meat in the henhouse, usually a hen that was not laying enough or a rooster that was mean or not doing his job very well. The table was running over with food from the garden or cellar.

"Those were the good days because the kids accepted with gratitude any small gift they might receive. They were expected to do their share of the work and chores, so Christmas was a very special day as they were excused from their daily chores and allowed to play with a toy and eat ALL day long. Cooking and eating were an important part of our lives at that time as food was the only thing we had in abundance.

"I shall always remember those Christmases on the farm, for I knew then, as I know now, how very, very hard my dear mother worked to make Christmas a happy and memorable day for her children."

THE LITTLE RED WAGON

Growing up on the farm homesteaded in 1891 by her grandfather, Zella Patterson has many memories of rural Christmases. The family land was eight miles from Langston, almost the same distance from Coyle, and 13 miles east of Guthrie, the county seat. After her father had proved the claim abandoned by *his* father, a treasured document was the deed signed by President McKinley. Zella, born in 1902, has lived all her life in the Langston area and has been associated many years with Langston University, for which she wrote the history.

"We never failed to have a Christmas tree, whether it was cedar or oak," recalls Mrs. Patterson. "In those days cedar trees were scarce in the area where we lived, and purchasing a Christmas tree was out of the question. Neighbors fortunate enough to have cedar trees on their farms were nice to share them. My father's Uncle George, who had staked out a farm at the same time Grandpa Black came to Oklahoma, had a number of cedar trees scattered over his pastureland and made us welcome to them. My parents felt we should not wear out the welcome and deplete his supply. They thought we should learn to be independent and do something on our own. Many times our parents would go with us in our own pasture to select a beautiful oak tree for Christmas that had not shed its colorful foliage. My mother would make some of the decorations and purchase some at the Kress variety store in Guthrie."

Preparations for winter, with Christmas included, took place all summer and fall on the Black farm. Summer fruits and vegetables were canned, preserved, and pickled; kraut was made; and during the Thanksgiving season Mrs. Black made fruit cakes and a huge supply of mincemeat pie filling, which she canned in jars. While she took care of these chores in the kitchen, her husband put sweet and white potatoes, turnips, and pumpkins in kilns of soil and collard greens in trenches to last the entire winter. Regardless of size or age, all five children were assigned responsibilities with this work. Prior to Christmas on a bitter cold day, a home-fatted hog was butchered and a large Christmas turkey from their flock was dressed.

Zella's parents shopped for Christmas early, purchasing gifts as well as ingredients for the Christmas baking. So much was raised at home, the shopping would be for sugar, flavoring, spices, brown sugar, salt, pepper, and cereal. Nuts and candy were purchased as well as oranges, apples, and bananas.

Back in those wagon-and-buggy days, it took two or three hours to drive to Coyle and several hours to Guthrie. The entire family would go to Guthrie at least three times a year, and sometimes Mr. and Mrs. Black would go while the children were in school. Each child saved change from his allowance during the entire year to do Christmas shopping at Kress' in Guthrie. A year's savings for each was usually under 10 dollars, but that would purchase more than 50 dollars in the present economy.

"One Christmas, about 1919, when my youngest brother, the baby of the family, was five years old, my parents had been to Guthrie quite early during the month of December," recalls Zella. "All of the children knew who Santa Clause was except our youngest brother, but our parents did not know we knew. While our parents went to Coyle in the wagon, my teenaged sister found the toys my mother had purchased for our baby brother."

Mrs. Black had carefully hidden the toys behind the living room *duofold*, or sofa bed in today's terms. When the young boy saw the little red wagon and other surprises due to be delivered by Santa, he declared that Christmas had arrived, and nothing could be done to pacify him when he was told otherwise. He was still in tears when Zella's folks returned home. Of course, he tearfully told his mother what had happened, and the others knew they were in big trouble: "We knew we would be punished for even touching things that did not belong to us. The guilty and not-guilty were reprimanded to a large degree."

Until then all five of the children, even the teenagers, had continued to hang stockings on Christmas Eve, retiring early so Santa would fill their stockings and leave gifts under the tree, but that tradition would be changed forever!

"Since you are so grown up and know so much," agreed both parents, "you need not hang stockings anymore. Since everyone is smart enough to know what they are going to get, from now on we will put up our tree and exchange gifts with each other instead of hanging stockings and waiting for Santa to put gifts under the tree. This goes for all *except the baby!*"

The lesson was never forgotten, and all because of a little red wagon!

MIXED EMOTIONS

"The most beautiful Christmas tree I ever saw stood in the little, one-room, white-frame Reorganized Church of Jesus Christ of Latter Day Saints in Ripley, Oklahoma. It was Christmas Eve, 1916," recalls Veneta Berry Arrington of Edmond.

"I loved this church with its big double doors in front and the cedar trees from the nearby bluffs planted around it. I particularly loved its windows. They were covered with a transparent tissue-like paper on each of which was printed a picture of Jesus. Even today I can see the dear, slender figure in its white robes, the gentle face, and the sweet little lamb held in His arms. The background was of grape vines with green leaves and purple grapes twining on a white trellis outlined in gold which sparkled when grey-bearded old Brother Cocamore lighted the coal oil lights or the sun shone through the panes just right.

"This Christmas Eve the glory of glories was the huge Christmas tree! Its fresh cedar fragrance filled the entire room. In my memory it reached the ceiling, and its full branches covered most of the west end of the church. The organ, with its red pump pedals, and the pulpit must have been moved to the side, for nothing obscured the view of this beautiful heavenlike apparition as my parents, brothers, sisters, and I came down the center aisle.

"The tree had red and green roping, strung popcorn, and a tinfoil star. But the miracle of miracles was the lighting. On the magnificent branches were seemingly hundreds of gently glowing, gently flickering lighted wax candles. Such heavenly splendor cannot be imagined unless one regains the eyes of a child. The candles had been attached to the branches in tin holders held in place with clamps of wood and wire springs (similar to clothes pins).

"The candles burned throughout the Christmas program. We sang. We prayed. We heard the story of Christ's birth read from the Bible. And all of us children got to speak pieces. I loved to speak pieces!" says Mrs. Arrington. "I stood up very straight and happy in my Christmas dress, which would be my Sunday dress for the rest of the winter. My dark hair, cut Buster Brown, was very clean, straight, and shiny. I spoke with eloquence, feeling my smiling parents' love: 'I'm a little girl three years old. Santa's coming to my house 'cause I'm just as good as gold!'

"After that, a few children got real Christmas presents. One girl got a lady doll with real hair and eyes that shut. We didn't mind because our mother explained that Santa Claus was going to leave our presents at our house. Besides, we already had found our dolls in their hiding place and had held them in our arms! Before we went home, we got sacks of delicious striped Christmas candy.

"As we left, we looked at the heavenly tree casting its magic spell so we would remember its beauty forever. I have never seen one its equal, and I am sure I never will.

"Possibly the reason for never seeing another tree like this was a tragedy we learned about when our weekly paper came. It told of a one-room church like ours with only front double doors and no rear exit—and a Christmas tree covered with lighted candles as ours had been. The tree had seemed to explode. Flames had darted to the ceiling. In their surprise and fright, the people had rushed to the doors to escape the flames, but the weight of their number held the doors tightly closed. Many had died that night in an awful tragedy.

"In our home it cast a shadow on our Christmas merriment. In our family prayers and at the table blessings, we prayed for the suffering and bereaved. Our parents taught us about Heaven, where we will be with our loved ones again and with our Heavenly Father, who loves us like little lambs.

"It was possible that this tragedy, the whereabouts I have forgotten, stopped the practice of lighted wax candles on Christ-mas trees. It was several years before electricity reached Ripley and other rural communities. It is strange that, through all these years that I have remembered this most beautiful Christmas tree which I have ever seen, I had forgotten the vicarious pain we felt because of the tragedy caused by a similar tree until I was asked to tell about a first Christmas tree."

Historical Note:

Although Mrs. Arrington finds the remembrance of these two events strange, their concurrence may be explained by the phenomenon of recalling two dramatic but independent events as one after a period of time. It is a common trick of the mind to blend two separate memories together. The tragedy she recalls may well have been the highly publicized Babbs Switch fire of Christmas Eve, 1924. At that time Mrs. Arrington would have been 11 and would have been more aware of news events than when she was three and had experienced her first Christmas tree.

The Babbs School, located near Hobart, was the scene of a typical Christmas program with a large tree bedecked with lighted candles and gifts. Reaching for a present near the top, Santa Claus, played by teen-aged Doug Bolding, pulled down a branch and touched it against a candle flame. Within moments the packed schoolhouse turned into an inferno in which 36 people were killed. News of the disaster spread through Oklahoma, having the same effect on other families that it had on Veneta Arrington's. 1924 was the last year for lighted candles on many Christmas trees in Oklahoma.

Table-top Christmas trees were popular throughout the Victorian era and as late as 1910, when this Oklahoma family gathered in the parlor with their small son and their display of gifts. Note the doll which the boy received. (Photo courtesy Western History Collections, University of Oklahoma Library.)

A SLEIGH COMES TO O.T.

Snow was swirling around outside the house as the children sat on the floor listening for the sound of sleigh bells. Grandpa had promised that if they stayed very quiet and still, the real Santa Claus would come with his sleigh and horses.

It was the turn of the century in Oklahoma Territory, and Ruth Cox Mc-Clanahan, now 90, recalls how excited they were when they suddenly heard bells ringing. There was a loud knock at the front door, and she remembers that all the children were too frightened to get up and go open it. When Grandpa threw open the door, there stood Santa himself! With a mixture of fright and delight, they assured Santa they had been good boys and girls. He filled their mother's largest dish pan with candy, and as he prepared to go he asked if any would like to ride in his sled. "No, siree, we will not," was the awestruck reply, but the children never forgot the invitation.

AMBROSIA FOR SANTA

The children in the family loved to watch Mama make the lovely Ambrosia, so delicious that its name was derived from the mythical food of the gods of Greek and Roman times. Little Marguerite Mitchener watched as her mother peeled and sectioned the fragrant, juicy oranges, which were available in markets only at Christmas time. Next her father, Dr. Mitchener, would split open the big brown coconut so Mama could drain off the milk and grate the sweet white meat. After she mixed the orange segments and the coconut, she usually added canned pineapple and sometimes a spoonful or two of sugar.

On Christmas Eve, Marguerite Mitchener McMahon recalls how Mama filled her beautiful cut glass bowl with the Ambrosia. So Santa Claus would not stumble in it and make a mess as he came down the chimney, the family placed the treat on the front porch. Most other children in the neighborhood put out cookies, and Santa surely was surprised to find Ambrosia when he arrived at Dr. Mitchener's big two-story house in Okmulgee, Oklahoma.

After the children had gone to bed, the Mitcheners brought the bowl in. This was a custom for many years during the period following statehood, and Christmas morning the curious children were amazed that Santa could consume such an enormous quantity of the wonderful treat.

PEPPERMINT FOOTPRINTS

All through the year, bits of tinfoil and colored paper were saved in the Bryan household in the Salt Creek-Wilson community seven miles north of Henryetta. Ollie Bryan Olson, now 82 years old, recalls the Christmas Eve ritual of bringing in a large hickory limb to be decorated and used as a Christmas tree. "Each limb was completely wrapped in green paper; then the tinfoil and other bits of colorful paper were used to decorate the tree," Mrs. Olson has told Bonnie Bolding of Midwest City.

One Christmas Eve the tree had been completed, and the children were in bed dreaming of Santa Claus when it started to snow. When the eight children awoke on Christmas morning, their father, Ben Bryan, told them to look out in the front yard and see Santa's footprints in the snow. Running out onto the porch, the excited children shouted and pointed at the large footprints engraved in the snow and heading straight for the Bryan house! The most amazing and memorable thing the children had ever seen—a large peppermint candy stick in each place Santa had stepped made a peppermint footprint for every child.

IN THE 1940s

"Some of my fondest Christmas memories were in Guthrie with my grandparents, who were 89ers. We gathered at Grandma Minnie Moore's about noon on Christmas Day, where a huge, sticky cedar tree found by Grandpa Jim on some farm nearby filled the small living room. Meagerly decorated with old tinsel and metal ornaments, its most memorable feature was the assortment of colored and different-shaped bulbs. I especially remember the Santa Claus bulb and ones shaped like a church and a little house," reminisces Sandra Bobzien of Oklahoma City. "Cotton was spread around the base of the tree. There were few other decorations around except when my uncle was away during the war [World War II]; then there was a banner with a star hung in the window. Because there were 14 of us, the presents for each person were small. Names had been drawn among the children and between the adults as well, and everyone kept secret the name he or she had drawn until Christmas.

"Hot rolls were rising on top of the refrigerator, and what a smell! The menu always included turkey, cornbread dressing, mashed potatoes, homegrown and canned green beans, orange jello with grated carrots and pineapple, and Grandma Minnie's own pickles and jams. Angel food cake and mincemeat pie topped it off. While the children played outside, the adults gathered around the dining room to play their favorite card game, pitch. Just as everyone recovered from the enormous meal, all the leftovers were set out for sandwiches, so all would return home contented."

SHOES FOR SAINT NICHOLAS

Children of the Maschino family laughed and chattered as they placed their shoes on the front porch, certain that in the night Saint Nicholas, patron saint of children, would pay them a visit. This was not taking place in Germany, where the legendary Bishop handed out gifts to "Kinder," but in Okarche, Oklahoma. Nor was it Christmas Eve, but the eve of Saint Nicholas' Day, December 6th, in the 1950s.

German customs have been continued by descendants of many settlers in the Okarche area, and Ann DeFrange recalls the pleasant mixture of European traditions with American ones. When children in her family put out their shoes for Saint Nicholas, they tucked letters with their requests to Santa Claus in the toes. During the night the sound of Saint Nick's boots could often be heard stomping around on the porch as he left his treats. Rushing out in the crisp December morning, Ann and the other children found nuts and hard candies—especially memorable was ribbon candy—filling the shoes. Her brother loved to find a *Blue Goose* orange still wrapped in tissue paper with the brand pictured on it. He treasured the juicy goodness of the fruit, so rare except at Christmas time. Gone were the letters to Santa Claus, whose mission would come on Christmas Eve.

Early on the evening of Christmas Eve, after the tree had been lighted and was ready for Santa's arrival, the children were herded out of the house on some contrived errand, perhaps a last-minute trip to the store or a visit to a relative's house. Returning home, they were thrilled to see that Santa had come. Toys were unwrapped, gifts exchanged, and a wonderful dinner served for the jovial celebration.

Christmas Day was reserved for Mass at Holy Trinity Catholic Church, where settlers had formed a parish in 1893. The beautiful brick church had been constructed in 1903 in the heart of the town. On Christmas Day friends and family visited one another in the close-knit community.

The Bill Maschino family still celebrates with a Christmas Eve dinner and fondly recalls childhood days when Saint Nicholas came all the way to the little town of Okarche, Oklahoma, to leave treats in children's shoes.

A NEW NATIVITY STORY

[*The following story is an account of a Nativity play presented on December 19, 1965, by children of the First Presbyterian Church in Norman. It first appeared in the* Norman Transcript *on December 20, 1965, and has been reprinted in newspapers all across the country. The story also won the Muchmore Award for the best news story in an Associated Press newspaper for its author, Jack Bagby.*]

A preschool version of the Christmas Story, complete with more than a few last minute improvisations, unfolded before a delighted audience at the First Presbyterian Church Sunday night.

The pageant of the Nativity, presented by members of the Cherub and Chapel choirs, in general had proceeded well at dress rehearsal. Mary, Joseph, the shepherds, wise men and other 4- and 5-year-olds in the cast had run more or less smoothly through their assigned parts. The Chapel Choir and a narrator provided the background, and except for minor entanglements with flowing robes and headdresses, few problems were encountered.

Then the Big Night arrived.

The first hint of trouble came even before the formal opening when one of the younger members of the Cherub Choir, a boy about 2½, took a fancy to the doll representing the infant Jesus lying in the manger. Clambering on stage he made a beeline for the crib and was diverted from his goal only by the action of an alert father.

The innkeeper, exhibiting a lively proprietary interest in the stable, practiced leaping about the freshly strewn hay until the arrival of Mary and Joseph, whom he escorted proudly to seats beside the crib.

The shepherds and white-robed angels arrived soon after. And it was then that the young Cherub, perhaps encouraged by his part as one of the children come to adore the Christ child, decided on another try for the object of his affections in the manger.

He squeezed his way through the crowd, grabbed the doll and lifted it from the crib. Mary, reacting like any mother, made a lunge for the swaddling clothes, and a tug of war ensued above the manger.

Joseph, stunned for a moment, gallantly came to Mary's aid with a swing at the intruder. And the innkeeper, proving not a bad sort after all, picked up a handful of hay and threw it at the would-be abductor.

The arrival of the harried father, towering some 3 feet above the rest of the cast, restored peace momentarily.

But it was all the hay, omitted during dress rehearsal, that caused the eventual downfall. Piled liberally about the tiled floor, it proved a lumpy and slippery footing. One of the shepherds, head bowed above the manger, suddenly went down. He scrambled up and immediately plopped down again. The third time he fell he grabbed the innkeeper; the inn-keeper bumped an angel and half the cast toppled like a row of dominoes.

But the hay provided a soft cushion—fun to dive into, in fact. Soon the shepherd and innkeeper were competing in swan dives into the straw. A wise man scuffled with an angel whose gilded wings had slipped con-siderably below their proper place. The Cherub, once more eluding his father, tried unsuccessfully to wrest a crook away from one of the shepherds.

The narrator and choir, unfazed by the commotion, continued like troupers to the end; the cast was enticed offstage and peace once more returned to the some-what disarranged stable.

One spectator, his voice still trembling with laughter, was heard to remark as he left the church: "I'm glad I read the Book, 'cause they sure changed the plot!"

Reprinted by permission.

TODAY'S TRADITIONS ARE TOMORROW'S MEMORIES

IN THE GOVERNOR'S MANSION

"In the three years we have lived in the Governor's Mansion, we have, in lieu of Christmas cards, had a 30-minute tele-vision special entitled 'From Our House To Your House.' We have used the time to introduce our family, share Oklahoma talent, and send Christmas greetings to all Oklahomans. Also for these three years we have had Open House at the mansion on a Sunday afternoon in December to show the Christmas decorations. This year the mansion was decorated for our son's wedding reception, which was December 19, 1981. Mike was married in the State Capitol Blue Room to Mara Kerr, grand-daughter of the late Senator/Governor Robert S. Kerr."

Mrs. George Nigh (Donna)
Governor's Mansion
Oklahoma City

SHOUT "CHRISTMAS GIFT!"

Coming from Kentucky to Bristow, Oklahoma, in 1912, Harry McMillan's family brought an enduring Southern tra-dition with them. The first time they see someone on Christmas morning, they give the person a kiss and say, "Christmas gift."

It is the first gift of Christmas and the most important to the McMillan family as it is a gift of love.

Other forms of this custom were found in many Oklahoma communities, where children tried to be the first to shout the magical words in order to collect a small token or gift. Little boys were the most ardent players of the game, and after family gifts were opened on Christmas morning, boys congregated on the streets of town showing off their presents and shouting "Christmas gift!" Ideally, the greeting was rewarded with a nickel or a stick of chewing gum, but sometimes pickings were poor.

Many years ago, when Marshall Stevens was a small boy in Vinita, he tagged along with a group of older boys as they hit the streets on Christmas Day to call out the unusual command for a gift. They were not having much luck when they spotted one of Vinita's more prominent citizens standing on the opposite corner. The mischievous fellows coerced young Marshall into approaching the judge. Reticently the youngster said, "Christmas gift, Judge."

The worldly gentleman understood the situation, knowing the older boys had put the terrified youngster up to the task. The judge reached into the pocket of his fine coat and drew out a shiny coin, "Here's a quarter, and don't give those guys across the street one cent of it."

Of course, he had to obey the judge! From that day forward, the boys in Vinita had new respect for little Marshall's skill at obtaining rewards from the holiday shout of "Christmas gift!"

Adapted in part from O.B. Campbell, Tales They Told (lithographed by Metro Press, Oklahoma City, 1977).

1889ers' CHRISTMAS ON THE HOMESTEAD

Most people decorate Christmas trees in December, but there is a group in Oklahoma City that gathers on October 31st for an annual tree-trimming party in the parlor of the 1889er Harn House Museum. This unusual group is made up of members of the 1889er Society, descendants of people who made the Run of '89 into the Unassigned Lands of central Oklahoma. They are dedicated to preserving the history and memorabilia of their pioneer ancestors.

As cold weather approaches, 89ers remove old-fashioned ornaments and antique toys from storage. Sitting around in the solid lap-sided and shingled Victorian Harn House, members of the organization string popcorn and cranberries the way their parents and grandparents did in earlier days. The only deviations from tradition are little crocheted candles instead of real ones [because of fire safety] and the substitution of an artificial tree for a real one because of the length of time it must stand in the museum for visitors to see.

Under the Christmas tree, a china doll reclines in a small, covered doll carriage, and antique wooden building blocks form a pyramid. An old china child's tea set is displayed on a hand-made, doll-sized washstand. A tiny washboard sits in a miniature galvanized washtub, and a child's rocking chair holds a worn copy of Clement C. Moore's "The Night Before Christmas." All the toys and furniture under the tree belonged to 89ers and have been treasured through the years as reminders of simpler times.

Throughout this typical 1904 farmhouse, special seasonal decorations are displayed. The kitchen, with its interesting assortment of implements, from apple peelers to butter churn, evokes memories of grandmother's Christmas baking.

William Fremont Harn built his house in 1904 on the 160-acre homestead northeast of Oklahoma City. He had come to the city in 1891 as a special agent for the federal land office, which settled land disputes and prosecuted illegal settlers called Sooners (anxious people who did not bother to wait for the sound of the gun at noon on April 22, 1889; they came early, made choice selections, then hid from patrolling soldiers, reappearing on the scene to stake claims the moment the land officially was opened).

In 1910, when the state's voters chose Oklahoma City as the permanent state capital, William Harn gave a portion of his homestead for part of the capitol grounds. The large, two-story frame farm house eventually was engulfed by residential development, and for years after Harn died

his niece, Florence O. Wilson, continued to live in the house at Northeast 16th and Stiles. In 1968 she gave the house and 10 acres to the city of Oklahoma City and the 1889ers Society, and after extensive restoration work on the house and grounds it was opened to the public as a museum in 1979.

Christmas visitors to the house see beautiful handmade quilts, a bread table shortened to accommodate a 4' 11" pioneer mother, and turn-of-the-century clothing of homestead style. Behind the house is a stone-and-wood contemporary version of the original barn, which burned down. Among displays inside the unique barn is an indoor water well with its windmill protruding through the roof. Children love to see the pump demonstrated.

A special exhibit of photographs lines one wall, a series of Christmas photos of two brothers as they were growing up. The earliest shows a baby on a rocking horse beside the family tree; others picture little boys in cowboy attire, and another has young men in World War I-style leggins. The photos have been developed from glass negatives donated to the museum by Donald and Elmer Akin, whose father was a professional photographer in early Oklahoma City. These rare candid shots give a glimpse of Christmas at home in that era.

The 1889ers who operate the Harn House Museum are proud of their pioneer ancestors, and the house and garden have been restored with obvious affection and respect. Chatting with visitors at Christmas time, some of them reminisce about their own families. Pau-

Professional photographer H. J. Akin took annual pictures of his two sons, Elmer and Donald, each Christmas as they were growing up. Donald, born in 1910, was a baby when he was propped up for his first Christmas picture; the bright light came from an open door at the Akin home at 7th and North Hudson. Each year a large tree was draped (sometimes vertically) with tinsel garlands, and the boys were showered with toys. (The original glass plate negatives for these photos were donated by the sons to the 1889er Harn Museum and Gardens. Never before published, the photos are courtesy 1889er Harn Museum and Gardens.)

*An Oklahoma
Christmas is...*

*Red in tones that move to brown,
Buildings that rise from orange clay,
Sun that bursts in a brilliant magenta,
Water that runs brown in the Cimarron River.*

*Straight in lines that merge together,
Plains plowed smooth when the wheat is in,
Oil rigs that pound in vertical motion,
Barns that lean in the strong south wind.*

*Dry, and windy, and cooler than usual,
Hunting season, and trees that are bare,
Blackjack, and oak, barbed wire, and thicket,
Roughhewn, and windblown, and spacious, and clean.*

*A manger that is a stall in the barn,
A shepherd that is an oil field worker,
Swadling clothes that are brown muslin bags,
And gifts that are wheat, and oil, and gas.*

*The Child, now as then,
Is our Hope, and our Joy:
So we invite you to join us
In the glad celebration that is...*

An Oklahoma Christmas!

SARAH JONES

Dr. and Mrs. Joe R. Jones

1982 is the 75th anniversary of Phillips University in Enid, as well as of the state of Oklahoma. President Joe R. Jones and his wife Sarah are native Oklahomans, and the pride they feel in their home state is evident in the 1981 Christmas card they sent to friends and family. Sarah Jones' original poem and the illustration by Jim Bray, Professor of Art and Director of Publications at Phillips, reflect their positive view of Christmas in northwestern Oklahoma.

line Lane, President of the Society, recalls a Christmas tree made by her father entirely out of telephone parts. He was very proud of it, and the family has kept it through the years. She also recalls her father's tales of the popularity of rutabagas during those early years. They produced such an excellent fall crop that everyone had them for Christmas dinner. Edna Couch recalls using a Red Haw tree for Christmas. The pretty red berries were edible—and made very nice, colorful decorations as well.

The Harn House at Christmastime offers a true step back into Oklahoma's Territorial homesteading days.

A SEASONAL THOUGHT

*How wonderful are fullest hearts at
    Christmastide
With gifts of love and season's cheer;
How much more wonderful if we could
    be
As full of love and charity
Each other day throughout the year.*
            —James Neill Northe
            (Our Sunday Visitor)

There is a lovely man in Oklahoma City who is a poet, philosopher, and, in his younger days, a musician. The remarkable James Neill Northe, used book dealer and authority on rare editions, is spending his 90th year sharing his positive philosophy of life through a vast correspondence. Anyone lucky enough to be on his mailing list has received inspirational Christmas cards, often with an original verse of the season.

A HOLIDAY GALA FOR AN ENTIRE CITY

"Something for everyone young and young in heart," was the theme for the first Holiday Gala given at the Marland Mansion in Ponca City in 1976. The citizens of the city made the purchase of the mansion possible by a special one-cent sales tax, which in only one year matched Continental Oil Company's pledge of $750,000. Because of this, planners for the benefit Christmas party wanted to insure that *everyone* who wanted to could come to the festivity.

As the event became an annual tradition, the Marland Mansion Preservation Committee has retained this philosophy. Money raised from the benefit is used principally for acquisiton of furnishings and their restoration. Strains of "Stardust" and "It Had To Be You" emanate from the ballroom where a big band plays for dancing. Although black tie is not required, local realtor and developer Lee Drake created a touch of nostalgia at the first Holiday Gala by wearing the tuxedo worn by his father at the 1935 inaugural ball of the builder of the house, E.W. Marland, Oklahoma's 10th governor. With the exception of pleats in the pants, the beautifully preserved garment compares with current styles.

Decorations are specially created by volunteers, sometimes Horizon Club members, Ponca High School art classes, and docents from the museum. Festive Mexican luminarios, made from paper bags filled with sand and a candle, light the border of the long driveway. Hundreds of ceramic, yarn, and bread-dough ornaments adorn the Christmas tree of the mansion. Many recreate designs from the tile floor of the recreation room of the house, and a star has been fashioned from a tile rubbing.

To appeal to local teenagers, the planners invite a guitarist and singer to entertain in a "coffee house" atmosphere on the third floor. At the same time a disc jockey spins records in the downstairs outer-lounge in a disco climate. Groups of friends cluster in upper-floor rooms to play their favorite card games, a popular activity for adults of the 1930s era.

E.W. Marland came to Oklahoma from Pennsylvania in 1907, the year of statehood, staying with the Miller brothers at the 101 Ranch until he struck oil in 1908 and moved into Ponca City. His fortune grew, and eventually he built a beautiful home on Grand Avenue, now the Cultural Center. Construction began on the grand estate in 1925, and for three years expert craftsmen worked to recreate the atmosphere of the Davazati Palace in Florence, Italy, out on a hilltop in the small town of Ponca City, Oklahoma.

In 1928 Marland moved in with his young, second wife, Lydie, but the dream was not to last very long. Strolls in the botanical gardens, fox hunts, polo games, swimming parties, and elegant balls ended abruptly in 1931 when the Great Depression hit E.W. Marland the way it had the rest of the country. He and Lydie moved out of the house, and within the next few years he sold his assets in Marland Oil Company to those who eventually would turn it into the tremendously successful Continental Oil Company (Conoco).

With the sale of his oil company, Marland turned to politics and ran successfully for Governor, serving from 1935 to 1939. Shortly before his death in 1941, he and Lydie sold their $5.5 million showplace to a group of Carmelite Fathers for $66,000. Within seven years the Fathers received $1.5 million for the property from the Felician Sisters, who eventually sold it to Ponca City for the same amount.

The Marland Mansion has been called *everybody's castle*. The Holiday Gala gives *the owners* an opportunity to celebrate the ongoing preservation and restoration of the house, dedicated in perpetuity for the enrichment of mankind as a cultural, educational, historical, and recreational center. Since its opening in 1976, it has been the scene of weddings in the chapel, wedding receptions under the vaulted, gold-leaf ceilings of the great hall, high school proms, business conferences, and the annual Renaissance Ball. Hundreds of tour groups are guided through regularly by volunteers.

Crowds up to 650 people have attended the Holiday Gala, sipping champagne and eating sandwiches next to the massive 10-foot pub table in the inner lounge or nibbling homemade cookies while seated in an original cane-back chair in the dining room. Guests feel a sense of pride as they consider the gift Ponca Citians have given their state. A number of those attending have donated or loaned furnishings of the 1920s period. Some pieces which have been given actually belonged to the Marlands, the donors purchasing them at the auction when the Marlands sold out. Now that the mansion is open to the public, visitors from all over the world express amazement that such an elaborate piece of architecture was constructed at such an unlikely spot.

Sounds of music and laughter waft on the December breeze to the stone gatehouse at the base of the hill next to the entry gates. Inside, Lydie Marland has returned to the estate after a self-imposed exile of more than 22 years. With her she brought some treasured pieces of furniture and lovingly replaced them in the exquisite setting created especially for her so long ago by her husband, E.W. Marland. Perhaps she listens to those happy sounds and recalls Christmases in the late Twenties when she was a young bride and hers was one of those joyful holiday voices.

AN INTERNATIONAL CHRISTMAS TREE

Each year when friends of Randy and Jimmie Fellers attend their annual Christmas brunch on the Sunday before Christmas, the first thing many visitors do is inspect the Fellers' international Christmas tree for new additions. Years of world-wide travel with the American Bar Association and the Oklahoma Zoological Society have brought a fascinating collection of ornaments from hundreds of places to their home in Oklahoma City.

DOLLS OF SPECULAAS

Not one Christmas setting but 14 fill the Stephens County Museum in Duncan when the holiday rolls around. Shortly after Thanksgiving Charlotte Jenkins, the museum's director, calls in the crew of volunteers who annually decorate the unusual array of Christmas trees. Each season they try to think of a new one to add to the collection. One tree with an Indian theme features Kachina dolls from the tribes of the Southwest. Another tree is laden with corn husk dolls, apples, and red velvet ribbons. Twinkle lights on the spectacular tumbleweed tree made by stacking up three of the circular weeds, are turned on only when visitors come. A local Girl Scout troop is proud of the typical pioneer Christmas tree—a scrub oak—which they decorated by wrapping the branches with green crepe paper and tying tinfoil gum wrappers on them.

In addititon to all the school groups making special Christmas visits to the museum, the general public has its special day with an open house featuring the trees, Christmas exhibits, and a boutique of handmade items.

Modern homemakers pay particular attention to a unique kitchen setting. Who would expect to find an antique German kitchen in the middle of southwestern Oklahoma? The centerpiece of the room is a hundred-year-old walnut cabinet, and displayed throughout the kitchen are original German cookie molds used to make Speculaas, a spicy cookie traditionally brought by Saint Nicholas to good boys and girls. The name translates as *mirror* because the cookie is the board's reflection after the dough is pressed firmly into the mold, then tapped out onto a pan for baking. Children visiting the Stephens County Museum at Christmas time are amazed to see cookies in the form of animals, rocking horses, and people molded from the hand-carved wooden boards. Some of the cookies were made by Mrs. Jenkins' mother more than 15 years before and are stored in airtight tins from year to year.

Many little girls beg their mothers to buy reproductions of the unique wooden molds sold in the museum shop so they can have *dolls of Speculaas* for their very own. Perhaps some have even made a Speculaas Christmas tree, hung in the German manner, with assorted cookies to be gobbled up as soon as Christmas comes!

TWELVE DAYS OF CHRISTMAS TREASURE HUNT

As soon as one holiday season is over, Dr. Jay Nelson starts planning for the next. Twelve months of creativity go into 12 days of fun for the four Nelson children. The object of his scheme is a treasure hunt over the 12 days preceding Christmas, and thinking of appropriate clues for each child's age and level of ability is a challenge Jay and Susie Nelson thoroughly enjoy.

On the first day the family gathers in the living room around a clue board containing 12 slots stapled shut and decorated with school pictures of the children. Each may have three or four color-coded—for easy identification—clues which will lead that child to something or some place. Tailored to each child, the clue might be in Morse code, a math problem, a verse from the Bible, or a phrase in a foreign language—anything fair and logical.

Examples:

Clue: Princess of England.
Solution: Margaret is the name of Susie's mother.

Clue: .5 & .5.
Solution: Look in the Half and Half container in the refrigerator.

Clue: Third Book of the Gospel.
Solution: Luke is Susie's father.

Clue: GDAOROARGSE or 1. I go up & down, 2. You pull me, 3. I'm part outside & inside.
Solution: Garage Door.

Clue: Greek N is pronounced, plus Z, REPAP.

Solution: Newspaper.

When the children were younger, clues led to small prizes, such as pencil sharpeners, ball and jacks, or a little game at the end of each day. The hunt has become more elaborate over the years with prizes like a pinball machine and a jukebox.

The Nelsons keep a record of all the clues and sometimes repeat one for a younger child. Although the clues take months to prepare, it is stimulating to Susie and Jay's imaginations, as well as their children's. All the Nelsons love these 12 days of Christmas and the Christmas treasure hunt they bring.

THE LUKES' SIGNATURE CLOTH

"Signing our red tablecloth used for Christmas dinner over the past 11 years has become a happy tradition for the Robert P. Luke family. Before the cloth is washed each year, the signatures and dates are embroidered in either green or white thread, so that when the cranberry spills are washed away the memories of the family gathered that particular year remain forever," reminisces Karen Luke. "The tiny, traced hand of a child too young to write, the shaky penmanship of a beloved grandmother now gone, and the happy drawing of a favorite sister mix with the signatures and dates to remind us each year of family love, which to us is so much of what Christmas is about."

A TRIBUTE TO AUNTY FANNIE

During Oklahoma's Semi-Centennial Celebration in 1957, Allece Locke's speech and drama students at Harding High School in Oklahoma City had a project entitled "Christmas in Oklahoma" in co-operation with the educational television channel. Now Allece is Mrs. Tom Garrard of McAlester, and serves as a member of the Diamond Jubilee Commission for Oklahoma's 75th anniversary.

For many years Allece and Tom have designed their own Christmas cards. A favorite, done in 1978, featured the portrait of a precious little old-fashioned girl (see photo). Inside was an explanation and greeting:

*The picture is of
Fannie Oliver
our beloved Little Aunty, now Ninety-Seven, who will wear a red dress and
come to our house on Holy Eve,
blessing our table as she blesses our
   lives.
"Dear Lord, we thank Thee for all
the gracious and wonderful blessings
of our lives and, Lord, we pray for
guidance in all those ways of right-eousness
and service for Thy sake.
Amen"
   We wish for you
   a long and happy life
and the Merriest Christmas ever*

Tom and Allece Garrard

THE BIG RED SLEIGH THAT CLANGS

When Old Town Museum was built in Elk City in 1966, it was on the edge of a quiet little town. Elk City has become a boom town with the exploration for oil and gas in the Anadarko Basin, and the museum has been engulfed by expansion. As the city has grown, so has Old Town's Old-Fashioned Christmas, held every year since 1971 on the first Sunday in December.

What began as a special event sponsored by Old Town Museum and the Western Oklahoma Historical Society has become a community celebration reminiscent of those held in frontier cities all over the Territories before statehood. More than 1000 modern pioneers converge on the park for the festivities.

Early in November Lucy Stansberry, Curator of Old Town, puts out a call for volunteers. Most of them have worked on the project before and are waiting for the fun to begin. Almost every organization and school in this new frontier city gets into the spirit of Christmas in the old-fashioned way.

Volunteers solicit donations of candy and bubble gum from all the merchants in town, and shortly before the event a group of parents have a sacking party to put candy in over 800 bags, one for each child expected to attend. Key Club members from Elk City High School spend Saturday putting up yards of green garlands on the front of the museum building and on the gazebo next to it, which is the focal point for Old-Fashioned Christmas. Lots of prayers are said that the garlands will survive the prairie winds which sweep across this part of the state at all times of the year. The students help Lucy put up two native cedar trees, annually brought from the Baker's Safari Ranch. One is tall enough to touch the ceiling of the gazebo in the center of the museum complex (the gazebo is one of the original structures built in the city-owned park). The other tree goes inside the museum.

Old-Fashioned Christmas draws the entire community together, and children of all ages bring handmade ornaments to place on the tree; Scout groups, Sunday School classes, and youth groups all participate. Entertainment is an important part of the celebration, just as it was in early frontier days. The high school band plays, members of the school chorus sing, and the highlight of the afternoon is usually the performance of the First Baptist Church Puppet Ministry. Hundreds of little people sit enraptured by the clever puppets as they act out an original Christmas tale. Laughter and fun is the order of the day, and the puppets provide the stimulus.

For many visitors, this is their yearly stop at Old Town, and they are anxious to see what is new at the museum: the Memorial Chapel, the one-room school house, the wagon yard, and the railroad depot (completed in 1981). Members of the Elk City Tsa-La-Gi Study Club volunteer as hostesses, showing people around the complex during Old-Fashioned Christmas.

Bells begin to clang, and little legs run out into Main Street just in time to see Santa Claus arriving in a big red fire truck. The excited children know he has treats for all of them. As the big red "sleigh" moves slowly down the street, young-sters scamper alongside shouting and waving to Santa. One very small girl turns to her mother and says, "I know that's the real Santa!"

"What makes you so sure?" asks her curious mother.

With wide eyes, the little girl looks up and says, "Because he said, 'Ho, ho, ho!'"

BABY STOCKINGS

Personalized, knitted Christmas stockings have been the welcome gift to many newborn babies whose parents were friends of Dr. Marion Smith and his wife Rachel in Stillwater. When the wee tot's first Christmas arrived, Santa found a precious stocking decorated with a tree and the baby's name and birthdate in which to deposit his or her first treats.

Over the years, as some of these special friends grew up and married, Mrs. Smith knitted stockings for the bride or groom of some of her "babies" from days past. The new family member's stocking included marriage dates, and now this tradition has extended into another generation as new babies arrive and grandchildren's stockings are made.

FEASTS WITH AN INTERNATIONAL FLAVOR

The annual Christmas Holiday Feast of a distinguished group of Tulsans who are members of the international gourmet society, Confrérie de la Chaine des Rotisseurs, always revolves around a continental theme. Whether a Victorian feast or an English Hunt Dinner, the dishes are carefully researched and planned, attentively prepared, and elaborately presented.

Mr. and Mrs. Robert Franden hosted a Christmas hunt dinner in their home in 1981 and selected dishes from all parts of the United Kingdom: Hunter's Game Pie, Fall Fruit Compote, Scrambled Eggs in Smoked Salmon, and Veal and Pork Pie. With these selections was served a variety of drinks: Pimm's Cup, Guiness Stout and Harp's Ale from Ireland, Gossip's Cup, and Chateau LaLagune haut Medoc 1976. The feast was concluded with Devonshire Cream and Currant Scones, English Trifle, and Scottish Shortbread. Finally Mr. and Mrs. Franden offered guests Stilton cheese and Harvey's Bristol Creme.

One of the most exceptional Christmas

dinners of the organization took place at Southern Hills Country Club, the scene for a Victorian Feast. Bailli (President) Kay Haggard has taken many trips into the English countryside, and for this special event Kay spent many weeks of research during an autumn stay in England. Her restaurant, Nicole's, in Tulsa, has an English pub atmosphere and is a favorite *watering hole* for Tulsans who appreciate fine food.

Invitations for the Victorian spectacular featured a charming Caldecott illustration of servingmen bringing in the Christmas boar's head, taken from Washington Irving's book, *Old Christmas*. In-side, the invitation offered an extensive menu for the evening. For the occasion Kay arranged to have the waiters and waitresses appropriately attired in Victorian livery, and Chef Rotisseur Donal Weaving prepared a boar's head, which preceded the main course in the manner of Caldecott's etching. The succession of sublime dishes created a masterpiece of taste, smell, and sight, and the five-hour excursion into Victorian England was an epicurean adventure.

Each year members are challenged to recreate traditional Christmas feasts of other countries equal in style and uniqueness to the year before.

TOYS UNDER THE TREE BEFORE CHRISTMAS

Visitors look quizzically at the toys under the Rhodes' tree in Ponca City and the Morrisons' in Edmond. Why would there be dolls and tractors *before* Santa's visit? The answer lies in Andrea Rhodes' and Judy Morrison's love of nostalgia.

Not wishing ever to part with her favorite toys, Andrea now uses them to decorate the area under her Christmas tree. The most treasured is her teddy bear all decked out in one of the many outfits Andrea's mother sewed for her fuzzy friend. Because she always loved the bear she received for her first Christmas, Andrea and her husband Jerry gave both of their children teddy bears on *their first* Christmases, too. Now all the bears congregate around the Rhodes' tree during holiday time.

The lovely old china doll resting under the native cedar in the Morrisons' Edmond home was the treasured possession of Judy's Grandmother Lewis. Beside it sit three of Judy's girlhood companions: a Toni doll brings back memories of the revolutionary Toni Home Permanents of post-war years when even little girls could curl their dolls' hair; a Madame Alexander doll of a "Little Women" character recalls the popularity of the Louisa May Alcott story among that generation; and a bride doll was a must for every girl in the Forties. Other things in the display have been gifts from Judy's sister-in-law, who makes delicate folk objects. The tractor and steam shovel with which Wes Morrison spent so many hours of his boyhood in Geary are now considered so-o-o old-fashioned by his two teen-aged boys—the vehicles are from the 1940s!

The large, bushy cedar tree represents a Morrison family custom of over 40 years. When Wes' parents, Mary Ila and Ward Morrison, were newlyweds, they went out to their pasture near Geary, where there was an abundance of cedars, and selected a Christmas tree. Every year thereafter, as their children were growing up, they did the same, and now Judy and Wes take their sons Ward and Todd to the same pasture on a Sunday before Christmas to chop the tree. Their *"old-fashioned"* toys complement the fragrance and fullness of the old-fashioned tree.

HAMPTON FAMILY OPEN HOUSE

Proclaim the Day of Christmas
and open now our door.
Come bring your family and
visit us once more.
Ring out false pride in
place and blood,
The civil slander and the spite.
Ring in the love of truth and right.
Ring in the family love so good.

Carol and Jim

Christmas Night
8 pm
December 25
1414 N. Hudson
Black tie optional

Thus reads the invitation sent out to friends of Dr. and Mrs. James W. Hampton. Each year, after all the gifts have been opened and the turkey consumed, more than one hundred of the Hamptons' friends gather in their fascinating Spanish Renaissance house in the Heritage Hills section of Oklahoma City. Entering the double doors, the first thing guests see is an enormous Christmas tree filling the three-story atrium that forms the entry hall and is the visual centerpiece of the 1913 home where Edna Ferber stayed while researching her Oklahoma novel, *Cimarron*. The live tree varies in size from year to year, but usually is 16 to 19 feet tall. It is placed on a special, moveable base which can be slid on the marble floor to the corners of the balcony. From the upstairs railing, Carol and Jim help their four children reach over to hang a collection of ornaments started over 20 years ago.

Greeting friends at the front door, Jim directs them to their choice of beverage: in the library is red or white wine; on the sideboard in the dining room is a tasty non-alcoholic punch; and on the massive dining table is the Hamptons' traditional Bourbon-Cranberry Punch. The table is lit solely by a large wrought-iron candleabra, which is surrounded by holly and red carnations.

Although everyone has had more than enough rich food during the weeks preceding Christmas, no one can resist Carol's exceptional buffet: smoked salmon, Brie pie, smoked turkey, and stuffed mushrooms.

Because the Hampton children range from grade school to law school, there is an interesting mix of age groups. While the older ones talk about their respective colleges all over the U.S., younger ones may be upstairs playing new Christmas games. Many parents who come to the annual party have been friends since childhood and look forward to the chance to reminisce once more about their own Christmases past.

THE PINE CONE LADY OF DUNCAN

Over the past eight years, Sheron Herndon has become the resident expert of Duncan, Oklahoma, on making pine cone wreaths. When friends admired the rustic-looking wreaths, she began to make them as gifts. The demand became so great that a local gift shop asked to carry them. Now on special occasions, Sheron will demonstrate her unusual technique to other women in the community as well as at her church, the East Church of Christ.

Each year as the holiday season approaches, Sheron gets out her year's accumulation of pine cones, peach pits, burrs, devil's claws, dried okra pods, dried burr flowers, acorns, and sliced and dried bois d'arc apples. Her family assists during the year by keeping sacks in the car so that wherever they might be, if some interesting natural materials appear, they are gathered. "My kids don't look up much; they're always looking on the ground trying to find something for me," Sheron says.

In addition to the natural decorations, assorted nuts are included in the list of supplies necessary to create the lovely, rustic look she desires for her wreaths. The only other supplies needed are wire, pans of water, and a heavy styrofoam wreath wrapped with heavy masking tape.

The water is the real secret of the success of her method, which is quite different from most (which call for toothpicks and glue). She dips each pine cone in water before wiring it to the frame. The trick was adapted from an observation she made on a Colorado camping trip with her family; there she noticed that the pine cones "closed up" when they became wet with dew.

"My system is to wire the things together while they are wet. Then when you are finished, you take the wreath out into the sunlight. After a couple of days it just billows up—it opens like a flower," she explains. "A wreath made this way is really strong. The wire makes it last longer, and the cones get fuller and stronger as they get older. The pressure of opening up causes everything to wedge in tightly."

Sheron recommends that any nuts or other materials gathered outdoors be cooked overnight in a 200° oven to kill the little mites that might take a liking to the wreath after it is completed.

A general pattern for the arrangement can be laid out before actual construction begins. Large and medium cones of varying color tones should form the outer edge, with smaller ones on the inside. The cones should be dipped in water a few at a time so they will not close up before they can be wired. Each then is wired individually onto the frame, alternately from inside to outside, with a *continuous* strand of wire. As pine cones are added around the circle, the first of the cones attached will close up from the moisture, leaving more room to layer. More are stacked up, squeezing them in as tightly as possible.

When the wreath seems full, she ties off

the wire. At this point, the extra materials become important for filling in small spaces. Her instructions are explicit: "Any place you can see through to the wreath, you take some of your other decorations, take a deep breath, and just cram them down in there until there is not a single solitary place to put anything."

The real fun begins when the wreath is laid in a sunny place to dry, and each day it changes, growing like a flower. As the drying cones open and expand, some of the small fillers may pop out. If so, Mrs. Herndon suggests, "You punch them back down. After about two days in the sun, you just put a dab of glue on anything that wiggles."

After the work of art has dried completely, there are optional ways to finish it out: some people like to preserve their wreaths with spray varnish for a shiny gloss, but Sheron Herndon prefers just an annual dousing of insect spray to retain a natural look.

With today's interest in the "country look" for decorating homes, the natural beauty of pine cone wreaths makes a charming addition to Christmas decorations of this style.

Adapted from the Duncan Banner, *December 4, 1981, by Sheila Dixon, Banner Lifestyle Editor.*

THE WHITES' CHRISTMAS TREE

A rustic contemporary house sits in the shadow of the enormous and imposing Marland Mansion in Ponca City. The young family living so close to the front gates of the mansion are on property originally part of the 2500 acres belonging to E.W. Marland, 10th governor of Oklahoma and renowned oil speculator of the 1920s.

Cheryl and Bill White are establishing their own traditions, as young families always have. The job of decorating the huge Christmas tree, almost tall enough to touch the cathedral ceiling of their country-style living room, always includes more than just their immediate family. Usually they invite another young family with chil-

dren and perhaps Bill's parents in Ponca City or Cheryl's sister from Tulsa, who brings her husband and little ones.

With all the children there, many of them under seven years old, Cheryl says, "It's usually wonderful chaos!"

The children are allowed to place the red satin bows and white lace on the tree at their discretion, and usually one side is loaded while the other is bare. The evening includes refreshments and lots of laughter as they make a party out of the White's Christmas tree. The following day Cheryl makes necessary adjustments to the placement of decorations on the tree so joyfully done by the little ones.

ZOO GREETINGS

"Seasons Greetings, OKC ZOO, Lawrence Curtis, Director, Oklahoma City Zoo and Staff," reads the inscription inside the special cards designed each year and sent to friends of the Zoo. A majestic lion poised between candles and holly brought kingly greetings one year. The charming countenance of M'Kubwa, the Zoo's renowned mountain gorilla, graced one of the more unusual cards another year.

AN EVENING AT THE OVERHOLSER MANSION

Hurricane lamps with flickering candles line the front walk, two huge evergreen wreaths dress the double front doors, and lights glitter from every window of the Victorian mansion. A lighted Christmas tree fills every window around the three-storied turret. It is the first Saturday night of December, and the Chafing Dish Society is holding its annual Holiday Buffet to benefit the Overholser Mansion.

As the doors swing open, the strains of a Strauss waltz drift from the antique music box in the music room. Laughter and conversation of the formally dressed guests fill the stately house. Now a museum, it looks the same as when Anna and Henry Overholser opened their new home to guests for the first time in 1905, christening the beginning of a social era unequaled in Oklahoma Territory. This realism is not the result of a clever restoration, but rather of careful preservation of the house and its contents by the two generations of family who occupied it.

The Overholsers' son-in-law, Jay Perry, maintained the fine structure after his wife's death until he could make satisfactory arrangements with the Oklahoma Historical Society and the Oklahoma Chapter of the American Institute of Architects to turn the home into a museum and preserve its priceless artifacts.

Often referred to as Oklahoma City's "first mansion," the Overholser house displays the opulence of crystal, rich fabrics, gold leaf, and rare woods from another age. The warmth and congeniality of the bristling new land in which it flourished is imparted to all who enter. Henry Overholser had left a lucrative business in Wisconsin to make the Land Run of 1889, after converting his assets into cash with which he bought pre-fabricated wooden buildings for shipment by rail to Oklahoma Territory. While other men were driving tent stakes, it was said he was building substantial frame buildings on the main streets of the young city, and when *they* moved up to wood *he* moved up to brick and stone, always one step ahead.

One of Oklahoma City's staunchest boosters, "Uncle Henry," as he was affectionately known, helped found the Board of Trade (later called the Chamber of Commerce) and was credited with once saving the State Fair from financial disaster. He also was influential in obtaining the State Capitol for Oklahoma City in 1910.

In 1901, just 12 years after the prairie had been opened to permanent settlement, Henry Overholser bought a piece of land far out of the city on Northwest 15th Street where the roads were unpaved, there were no trees, and the land was a virtual cow pasture. Several prominent men established Highland Park as a showcase of beautiful homes to reflect the positive growth of the city.

An English architect supervised construction of the turreted house of buff brick and Pecos Valley brown stone. The best artisans and craftsmen were retained, including a graduate of the Kensington Art School as decorator. Construction, begun in 1903, was not completed until 1905, at which time skeptical friends claimed, "No one will ever be able to get out that far." But those very skeptics were the first to arrive in their carriages when the Overholsers held their open house in the chateau-type mansion.

Oklahoma City's first bridge and social club, the Monday Chafing Dish Club, held frequent meetings here. Organized in 1899, the club reflected the exuberant character of the time and became a prime planner of the city's social activities. The original 21 members chose their name *to enlarge on the fashionable manner of intimate dining* at the turn of the century, that of serving a one-course feast from a chafing dish.

Charter member Anna Overholser was a frequent hostess, with as many as 500 guests for special events of the Chafing Dish Club, like fashion shows, teas, dinner parties, and lectures.

Guests at the annual Chafing Dish Society Holiday Buffet have the same sense of awe and grandeur as those first guests so many years ago. With the additional wonder of age and careful preservation, visitors have been heard to exclaim, "I have the eery feeling of having stepped back in time."

At the east entrance on Hudson Street, party-goers are greeted by Anne and Tom Flesher, annual hosts. Behind them is the great winding staircase of dark oak wrapped with evergreen garlands. One can imagine the beautiful Anna descending the stairs to greet the evening's callers in her elaborate gown with its customary flowing train. Candles and poinsettias fill the entry hall, and in the cupola under the stairs is the old-fashioned Christmas tree.

The front parlor is resplendent with pieces of Meissen and Dresden. The walls and ceiling are still covered with the original hand-painted canvas which took a live-in artist several months to create. There always is a very special Christmas tree in the parlor for the Chafing Dish party, once a gigantic "tree" made of tiers of bright red poinsettias. Another year a green tree was decorated with numerous miniature hot air balloons fashioned of papier-maché by Mrs. Wendell Locke, a member of the AIA Auxiliary.

Jean Gumerson recalls how she and her late husband, Dow Gumerson (then chairman of the committee working out plans for purchasing and running the house), came up with the idea for raising funds: "We were looking through the old Overholser scrapbook, which still sits on the hall table, and read about the Chafing Dish Club and all the events they used to have here, so we formed the Chafing Dish Society after the old club."

Membership in the Society costs $1000. The first $50,000 raised was matched by federal funds to purchase the property, and additional donations were used for renovations. To honor those first donors, an afternoon reception was held on the first Sunday in December, 1972. That was the beginning of a tradition which has evolved into a festive evening buffet attended by 250 people.

Guests mingle throughout the charming home. Next to the parlor is the gold music room, furnished with Louis XV and XVI gilt furniture and *haunted* by musical performers of the past who entertained on the fine grand piano.

"One Christmas the Society invited a harpist to perform. Another time Victorian carolers straight out of Dickens' *Christmas Carol* appeared in costume from the Oklahoma Theatre Center (where the play is performed each Christmas). "Dinner guests were delighted," recalls Dannie Bea Hightower, another party organizer and neighbor. (Frank J. Hightower's grandfather built their Classic Revival house three doors west shortly after Overholser).

Back out in the east entry hall, the visitor is drawn up the oak staircase by two lovely Grecian girls playing musical instruments. They have stood at the first landing since 1905, and will remain as long as the house survives. They are exquisite creations of stained glass—two maidens in flowing gowns, one holding a violin, the other a tambourine. For 75 years vehicles have stopped on 15th Street so passengers could gaze at their beauty.

A few steps up on the second landing is the masterpiece of Christmas trees ever displayed at the party—the storybook tree. For this tree Willie Locke created wooden ornaments depicting all her favorite childhood tales in miniature scenes, including "The Little Engine That Could," "The Three Little Pigs," and "Rub-a-dub-dub, Three Men In a Tub."

The upper hall is filled with more red poinsettias, and it is easy to see how 500 of the plants are required to decorate the house each year.

Down in the dining room, with its crystal chandelier and dark oak furniture, a feast awaits the guests—a typical Southern Christmas buffet of ham and turkey, green bean casserole, cheese grits souffle, pickled black-eyed peas, and pecan and lemon tarts. A magnificent arrangement of red carnations and holly fill Mrs. Overholser's cut glass bowl, and candlelight gives a soft glow to the silver chafing dishes.

People sit all over the mansion to eat dinner: in the library filled with oriental antiques, on the back stairs, or in the upstairs sitting room. Across the hall from the sitting room is a bedroom which has been transformed into a 1906 nursery by the Colonial Dames. Mrs. O. Alton Watson spent hours restoring and arranging childhood mementos of the Overholsers' only child, Henry Ione, and of other neighborhood children. In a closet nook in the hall, Mrs. Watson fashioned a photo gallery of neighbors from the era.

As the candles burn down and the buffet is cleared, the crowd thins as older guests head home and younger ones continue on to other parties. Once again the 16 rooms of the old mansion, with its precious store of antiques, becomes a hall of unspoken memories. It seems fitting that once more, if only for one festive Christmas evening, the Overholser house breathes again and experiences merriment—as it did when Oklahoma was young.

FOUR TREES SHINING

Four lighted Christmas trees illuminate the large double windows of the Southern Colonial home and announce to passersby that Christmas season has arrived in Stillwater. The children who first placed trees in these windows have grown up and left, but the tradition continues.

The custom began with a trip to the farm of their grandfather, Harley Thomas, member of an early pioneer family. With great care, each youngster selected a perfect tree. Decorated with ornaments made at school, the tree in each child's room was the place for sibling gifts. Visiting each other's rooms to open the gifts on Christmas morning kept them busy while *Santa* donned his red, furry cap, lit the fireplaces, and turned on Christmas music. The excited children were not allowed downstairs for Santa's surprises until they paused on the staircase for annual photos.

Virginia and Bill Thomas, Mayor of Stillwater for many years, still place trees in the upstairs windows on behalf of their children for the enjoyment of their many friends who look forward to this first sign of Christmas.

CHRISTMAS EVE CANDLELIGHT SERVICES

Church is still the most important part of Christmas for many modern Oklahomans, and as family traditions have evolved so have church traditions adapted to change. Christmas Eve services in many churches have become principally religious rather than secular (with the tree celebrations so popular in territorial days). Now most families have their own Christmas trees at home, and they look to the church for the true meaning of the season, the birth of Jesus Christ.

One of the most beautiful events is an early evening communion service at Chapel Hill United Methodist Church in Oklahoma City where more than 80 bright red poinsettia plants decorate the chancel. Because so many young families with children attend Chapel Hill, Reverend Jim Rodgers has a series of 30-minute services from 5:00 to 7:00 p.m. "to allow families to touch base with the church in the midst of their busy schedules." The reading of the scripture, the brief communion, and two vocal solos are presented in the semi-darkness of the large contemporary sanctuary. At the close comes the singing of a Christmas carol, so familiar that parents and children need no hymnal—usually the choice is the beloved "Silent Night."

A mile away, at Village Methodist Church, a Carol and Candle Service has become a tradition. Members gather for an hour to sing carols and hear the scriptural versions of Christ's birth. In Edmond the warm tones of the wood-beamed ceilings in the old sanctuary of First United Methodist Church and the stained glass windows lighted from the outside for the evening service lend an old-fashioned air to the Christmas Eve communion.

Midnight services at First Presbyterian Church, St. Paul's Episcopal Cathedral, and All Souls Episcopal Church, all in Oklahoma City, draw many non-members because of the beauty and magnificence of their traditional services with full choirs and inspirational atmosphere.

The midnight service at First Presbyterian Church in Tulsa features wonderful Christmas music. Janie Barnes Sneed, whose vocal talent is widely known, has often been featured, and now her three children join in the family tradition also as soloists with the choir at Christmas.

Because early traders and missionaries among the Osage Indians of northern Oklahoma were Jesuits, the Catholic Church converted many members of that tribe. Today in Pawhuska many descendants of those early converts gather for Christmas Eve Mass at their Catholic Church.

The manger scene is set in place in front of the altar at St. Andrews Episcopal Church in Stillwater. As the little children approach the *stable*, they gaze in wonder at the doll-sized baby Jesus. They have gathered at a special children's Christmas service the afternoon of Christmas Eve to experience what the Wise Men did in giving a gift to the Christ child. Each youngster brings something that is precious to him or her to leave for Jesus, learning the true meaning of giving. When the parents, grandparents, and older brothers and sisters attend Christmas Eve service later that night, they smile when kneeling to take communion as they survey the gifts left that afternoon—a worn out baby blanket, a baby doll, a stuffed animal, and even a Star Wars doll.

As the last hymn is sung in the darkened First Presbyterian Church in Bristow, the Advent candle is used to light a candle held by each person in the sanctuary. Row by row, the flame is passed to the next person until the church is bright with candlelight. In an inspirational procession, everyone files out of the church into the Christmas Eve night carrying the light of Jesus Christ out into the world.

PART III

CHRISTMAS DELIGHTS
FROM THE KITCHEN

Gingerbread house, instructions, page 116. (Illustration by Judy M. Samter.)

During the holiday season a most special restaurant to visit with friends or out-of-town company is the Roosevelt Grill in Edmond. The sophisticated elegance of the relatively new restaurant is especially appealing at this time of year. Although served at other times, Brie Soup is particularly good with a holiday meal, and Chef Linda Trippe gets many compliments on it.

BRIE SOUP

1 pound Brie cheese
4 shallots, minced
2-4 cloves garlic, minced
White part of 1 leek, sliced (optional)
¾ cup butter
¾ cup white flour
4 cups mushrooms, sliced
4 cups California cream sherry
4 cups beef broth
Heavy cream
Kosher salt
White pepper
1 leaf thyme

Set cheese out to ripen at room temperature. Chop shallots, garlic, and leek in food processor. Saute butter until soft over medium heat. Add flour and cook until blond roux. Add mushrooms and set aside. In another saucepan, brown the alcohol out of the sherry until there is no longer a flame and add beef broth. Bring sherry and stock to boil, then slowly whisk in mushroom mixture. Add heavy cream to desired thickness and season to taste with salt, pepper, and thyme. Serve over a wedge of the soft Brie. A California Fumé Blanc or Pinot Noir will accompany the flavor of the soup well.

Linda Trippe
Edmond

NUTS AND BOLTS

1 small box Corn Chex
1 box Rice Chex
1 box Wheat Chex
1 box pretzel sticks
1 pound mixed nuts
3 sticks margarine, melted
2 T. Worcestershire Sauce
2 tsp. Tobasco Sauce
2 tsp. garlic salt
2 tsp. savor salt

Mix sauces, salts, and margarine. Pour over dry mixture and toss well. Bake at 250° for 1 hour, stirring at least twice.

Dorothy Kennedy
Oklahoma City

Christmas Eve in Oklahoma may mean piping hot bowls of homemade Chili, as it does for the Arthur E. Peters family. Ever since Sybil was a little girl growing up in Pawhuska and Tulsa, she remembers her mother making a big pot of the spicy Southwestern dish. Because it is easy to prepare and serve, there is more time for the Christmas Eve gift exchange. Then on Christmas Day a large turkey dinner is served. They still adhere to this tradition with their two sons and daughters-in-law.

CHILI

2 pounds hamburger meat
1 T. shortening
½ onion, chopped
2 T. chili powder
1 #2 can tomatoes
Salt and pepper to taste
1 T. cumin
1½ cans water

Brown chopped onion in shortening. Add meat and brown. Stir in chili powder, salt, and pepper. Run tomatoes through a sieve and add to meat mixture. Stir in cumin and 1½ cans of water (using tomato can). Cook slowly for 2½ hours. Serve with crackers, Picante pepper sauce, and chopped hot peppers.

Sybil and Art Peters
Oklahoma City

A member of the pioneer Oklahoma City Blake family, Eleanor Kirkpatrick recalls spending family Christmases with her cousins, the Bakers. Three first cousins had the Baker-Hanna-Blake Wholesale Drygoods Company. "Mrs. Joseph F. Rumsey was the Baker daughter, and it was at her home that we gathered for Christmas dinner. She always had a large live Christmas tree with lighted candles. My favorite dish that she served was escalloped oysters."

ESCALLOPED OYSTERS

Place raw oysters in a large casserole. Crumble saltine crackers on top and dot with butter. Pour some cream over them and bake in a 350° oven until they are cooked and the crackers are slightly browned, about 30 minutes.

Eleanor Blake Kirkpatrick
Oklahoma City

BLUE CHEESE IN CRUST

2 packages (10 oz. each) frozen puff
   pastry patty shells
1 egg beaten
½ pound blue cheese, crumbled

Remove shells from package; let stand at room temperature until slightly softened. Stack 6 shells; roll out on a floured board to a 12 x 5 inch rectangle. Trim edges with a knife or pastry cutter to make rectangle even. Save trimmings. Place on ungreased cookie sheet. Brush edges with egg. Place cheese on pastry, leaving a 1-inch border free of cheese on all sides.

Stack and roll remaining shells to 12 x 6 inch rectangle. Trim if necessary and save trimmings. Place on top of first part. Press edges together to seal them. (Recipe may be prepared to this point the day before. Chill. Let stand at room temperature 15 minutes before proceeding.)

Brush pastry with beaten egg. At Christmastime the trimmings may be used to form a simple Christmas wreath on top of the pastry. Color the wreath by brushing red or green food coloring on with a watercolor paint brush. Make a bow, too.

Bake at 425° for 30 minutes or until puffed and golden brown. Let stand 15 minutes before serving. Cut in 1-inch slices. Makes 12 servings.

Sheila Dixon
Duncan

Quail has replaced traditional birds among some Oklahomans for the Christmas feast. The delicate flavor and specialness of the game bird have made it popular since earliest territorial days. Ronald E. Rosser has always supplied the birds for a Christmas Eve candlelight quail dinner, and his in-laws, the E. Lee Kennedys, especially enjoy it since Lee is not a hunter. Wild rice and Oklahoma sand plum jelly are served with the quail.

Susan Barnhart Wade grew up in the country north of Oklahoma City where quail could be heard calling and the supply was plentiful at Christmas time.

QUAIL

Soak cleaned quail overnight in buttermilk. Shake in plastic bag with flour, salt, and pepper. Brown on both sides in iron skillet in hot shortening (or butter). Place in baking dish, cover, and bake at 350° for about 25 minutes.

Susan Wade
Oklahoma City

Many first-generation Czechs came to America and on into Oklahoma Territory before statehood, settling various parts of the area and plying varied trades and professions. Named after the historic capital of Bohemia, Prague, Oklahoma was populated by these early-day Czechs, as were Yukon, Wheatland, Perry, and parts of Oklahoma City. George Miskovsky, Sr.'s parents came to Oklahoma at that time and brought the customs of old Bohemia, where at Christmastime they always served roast goose filled with sauerkraut stuffing and bread dumplings (*Pecena Husa se Zelim* and *Huskove Knedliky*). Mr. Miskovsky, a true epicure, prepares the tradititonal Bohemian goose for his family each Christmas.

PECENA HUSA se ZELIM
(Roast Goose with Sauerkraut)

An 8-10 pound goose
1 cup water
4 pounds fresh, canned, or packaged
   sauerkraut
2 cups finely chopped onions
1 cup grated raw potato
2 cups finely chopped apples
½ tsp. salt
1 T. caraway seeds
Freshly ground black pepper
Salt

Preheat oven to 325°. Pull out all loose fat from inside goose and dice fat into ½ inch chunks. In small saucepan, simmer fat with a cup of water, covered, about 20 minutes. Uncover and boil liquid completely away. Fat will begin to sputter. Continue cooking until sputtering stops. Strain fat into a bowl and reserve. Discard browned fat particles.

Drain sauerkraut, wash it well under cold running water; then, to reduce sourness, soak in cold water 10-20 minutes. Squeeze dry by the handful. Heat 6 tablespoons of the goose fat in a heavy 10- or 12-inch skillet and add the onions and sauerkraut. Stirring occasionally, cook uncovered about 10 minutes. Transfer the sauerkraut mixture to a large mixing bowl. Add the apples, potato, salt, caraway seed, and a few grindings of pepper.

Wash goose inside and out with cold running water, pat it dry with paper towels, and sprinkle the cavity generously with salt and a few grindings of pepper. Fill the goose with the sauerkraut stuffing, sew up the goose, place breast-up on a rack in a large roasting pan. Cook in the middle of oven for 2-2½ hours, or 20-25 minutes per pound. With a bulb baster, occasionally remove the grease that drips into the pan. The goose is done when the juice from a punctured thigh runs pale yellow.

When the goose is done, remove it to a serving platter and cut away the thread and cords. Transfer the stuffing to a serving dish. Let goose rest on the platter at least 15 minutes before carving. Serves 6.

HOUSKOVE KNEDLIKY
(Bread Dumplings)

4 T. butter
3 cups ½-inch bread cubes
3 T. finely chopped onions
10 T. flour
2 T. finely chopped parsley
½ tsp. salt
⅛ tsp. nutmeg
¼ cup milk

Melt 3 tablespoons butter in heavy skillet. When foam subsides, add bread cubes. Toss about in butter until they are brown on all sides. Set aside.

Add rest of butter to the skillet and, when melted, stir in onions. Cook 3-4 minutes until they are lightly colored, then scrape them into a large mixing bowl. Stir in the flour, parsley, salt, and nutmeg, and moisten with the milk. Knead lightly to form a dough. Gently fold in the bread cubes and let the mixture stand for about 30 minutes.

Divide dough in half, knead with your hands, and form into 2 long, sausage-like rolls about 2 inches in diameter (about 5-7 inches long).

Carefully place the rolls in an 8-inch saucepan half full of boiling salted water. Cook gently over medium heat 20-25 minutes, turning them once with a large spoon or 2 slotted spoons. Remove them to paper towels to drain. Cut them into ½ inch slices while hot. Serve with the goose.

George Miskovsky, Sr.
Oklahoma City

The Peters family of Edmond is descended from two pioneer families who settled in the area shortly after it was opened for settlement. They still expect to find homemade noodles, prepared the way their mother made them, on the Christmas table with the turkey.

NOODLES

1 cup flour
1 whole egg
½ tsp. salt
½ of an eggshell of cream or canned milk

Mix and roll out on a floured board. Cut in strips with a noodle cutter or thin knife. Lay on a floured newspaper to dry. (My sisters and I still use newspaper because that is what Mama always used, and it works just fine.) When well-dried and slightly brittle, cook in chicken broth uncovered until tender, about 20 minutes.

Patsy Peters Miller
Edmond

When Barbara Stanfield came to Oklahoma, she had never tasted cornbread dressing, so popular all through the South. It seemed bland compared to the spicy Turkey Dressing made with sausage, which she had grown up with in Montana and which has now become a tradition with her family at Christmastime in Oklahoma.

TURKEY DRESSING

½ pound mild sausage
½ pound hot sausage
½ pound butter
1 pound loaf bread, dried, toasted, and
   rolled into crumbs
½ onion, grated
1 egg
1 cup chopped celery
1 cup sliced mushrooms
1 tsp. poultry seasoning
Salt, pepper, and celery salt to taste

Brown all the sausage and pour off grease. Add butter to sausage. Mix remaining ingredients and toss together with the sausage mixture. Break in one egg and mix with a fork. Add boiling water (and wine, if desired) until moist. Toss with a fork. Fry until brown, and fill turkey cavity with it before roasting.

Barbara Stanfield
Oklahoma City

"When our children were very small and their friends came over on Christmas morning to compare toys, the little guests often stayed for breakfast. This grew into a neighborhood brunch with parents included, along with friends who had no families with whom to celebrate."

CHEESE GRITS SOUFFLE

2 cups hominy grits
1 stick butter
2 tsp. salt
2 T. savory salt
1 pound sharp cheese
3 eggs, well beaten
10 drops Tobasco sauce

Cook grits according to directions omitting salt. When done, add butter, salt, savory salt, and cheese (melts faster if it has been cubed or grated). Beat eggs very well and fold into grits, then add Tobasco. Bake at 350° for 40 minutes.

Virginia Thomas
Stillwater

When Kay Haggard opened her restaurant in Tulsa in August, 1977, she wanted it to recreate the atmosphere of the little cafes and bistros she had often enjoyed in England and France, not only in the food but also in the decor. Through careful planning, Nicole's Cafe Bistro has achieved that. The wood paneled walls, the delicate etchings, and the country prints of the wallpaper and fabrics give the patron a sense of stepping from the sidewalks of Utica Square into a European cafe. The food is light and fresh, with a constantly varied menu. During the cold Christmas season, these Scalloped Potatoes are a popular and hearty addition to their selection of entrees.

NICOLE'S CAFE BISTRO
SCALLOPED POTATOES

2 pounds white potatoes
2 cups milk
2 cups heavy cream
1 large garlic clove, minced
¾ to 1 cup Gruyère cheese
1 tsp. salt
1 tsp. paprika
1 tsp. white pepper
1 T. butter

Heat oven to 350°. Peel and slice potatoes ⅛ inch thick. Place in saucepan, add milk, cream, garlic, and seasonings. Bring to a boil, stirring constantly. Boil for two minutes.

Butter baking dish. Spoon in the potato mixture; sprinkle with cheese. Bake about 1 hour. Reduce heat if browning too quickly. Serve hot or cold.

Kay Haggard
Tulsa

SWEET, SWEET POTATOES

6 large sweet potatoes
3 eggs
¼ tsp. nutmeg
¼ cup milk
2 T. cinnamon
3 T. butter
⅛ tsp. cloves
1 tsp. salt
½ cup sugar
Marshmallows

Bake and peel potatoes. Mash them and add eggs, milk, and butter. Add the remaining ingredients. Pour into a casserole. (This can be done ahead and frozen.) Bake at 350° for 1 hour. Cover top with marshmallows and put under the broiler until lightly browned, approximately 5 minutes.

Peggy Haynes
Edmond

"My mother and father, my only sister, and I have lived in Oklahoma City since 1937. It is our custom to be together on Christmas Eve with friends to share our blessings with them. On Christmas Day, we travel to all three trees and alternate where we have breakfast and Christmas dinner. Along with the traditional turkey, this Broccoli Casserole has become an annual favorite."

BROCCOLI CASSEROLE

2 pkgs. frozen broccoli
2 T. flour
6 T. butter
¼ cup chopped onion
3 eggs, well beaten
½ cup water
1 16-oz. jar Cheese Whiz
½ cup cracker crumbs

Saute onions in 4 tablespoons butter until soft. Make a paste of flour and water and pour into onion mixture. Cook until thick. Cook broccoli, drain, and combine with onion mixture. Add half of the crumbs and the jar of cheese. Mix gently with the eggs. Put into a greased casserole, dot with butter and the rest of the crumbs. Bake at 350° for 20-25 minutes.

Betty Lou Fritsche
Oklahoma City

MUSHROOM-ONION CUSTARD

½ pound mushrooms
1 Spanish onion
½ pound sharp cheddar cheese
¼ cup butter
1½ cups salted cracker crumbs
⅓ cup melted butter
½ tsp. curry powder
3 beaten eggs
1½ cups scalded milk
½ tsp. salt
Dash cayenne pepper
Cherry or plum tomatoes (optional)

Slice cleaned, fresh mushrooms lengthwise. Thinly slice the peeled onion. Grate cheese. Cook mushrooms and onion in ¼ cup butter for 5 minutes. Thoroughly blend coarse cracker crumbs, melted butter, and curry powder. Line a 12 x 8 inch buttered baking dish with the crumb mixture. Beat eggs well. Blend mushrooms, onion, and cheese with eggs, scalded milk, salt, and a dash of cayenne. Pour vegetables and cheese mixture into crumb-lined dish. Bake at 350° for 1 hour or until custard is set. Top each serving with tomato in last 15 minutes of baking if desired. Serves 8-10.

Dorthlynn Gaddis
Oklahoma City

"We always have an absolutely marvelous Christmas with lots of mistletoe and holly and a huge live tree with decorations from trips we have made all over the world and ones Walt and I had as children. The huge Christmas dinner includes Walt's mother, Mrs. W.W. Woolley, a delightful lady of 91, who always comes to share the day with us. Our four daughters, ranging in age from 21 to 28, still hang stockings on Christmas Eve, and Santa still fills them! To all of us, Christmas Day is the most meaningful of the year, a time of love and celebration."

ANN'S CHRISTMAS SALAD

2 pkgs. strawberry Jello
2 cups boiling water
1 pkg. frozen strawberries
3 bananas, mashed
1 16-oz. can crushed pineapple
¾ cup nuts
1 8-oz. carton sour cream

Mix Jello and add fruit. Place half of the mixture in a three-quart casserole. Let Jello partially set in refrigerator. Spread a layer of sour cream over it and put rest of Jello mixture on top. Refrigerate.

Ann and Walter Woolley
Ada

The same year Oklahoma celebrates its 75th anniversary of statehood, Inez Poarch of Crescent celebrates her 90th birthday. For many years she has made this fresh cranberry relish at Christmas for family and friends.

FRESH CRANBERRY RELISH

1 pound pkg. cranberries
1½ unpeeled oranges
¼-¾ cup sugar

Wash and cull the berries. Wash and quarter the oranges, leaving peeling on; remove seeds. Grind the berries alternately with the oranges with a meat grinder, using a glass baking dish to catch the fruit and a larger pan underneath to catch errant juice. When grinding is completed, combine the two. Sweeten with sugar to taste. Pack in airtight containers and let age in refrigerator for two days. It also can be frozen. It keeps well in the refrigerator for 2-3 weeks and can be made in very large quantities.

Anita Poarch
Edmond

CHRISTMAS SALAD

1 pkg. unflavored gelatin
¾ cup cold water
1 15½-oz. can crushed pineapple
1 small bottle red maraschino cherries
3 or 4 candied dill strips
¾ cup pecans or walnuts
1 small can pineapple juice
½ cup sugar

Soften gelatin in water. Chop cherries, dill strips, and nuts. Mix pineapple juice and sugar; boil for 3 minutes. Add the softened gelatin to the sugar syrup and cool slightly before adding the rest of the ingredients, including the juice of the cherries. Chill in refrigerator. This is especially pretty at Christmas because of the red and green ingredients.

Lyntha and Allan Muchmore
Ponca City

This Cranberry Salad recipe belonged to Lois McMillan's husband's grandmother, Mrs. Harry Ekdahl. The only modernization is a food processor to grind the cranberries.

CRANBERRY SALAD

1 quart cranberries
1 cup sugar
2 cups hot water
1 small pkg. lemon Jello
15 marshmallows
1 cut apple, peeled and minced
1 cup celery, chopped
1 cup nuts, chopped

Grind cranberries, add sugar and water. Boil 5 minutes. While hot, add Jello and marshmallows; stir until dissolved. Cool, then add apples, celery, and nuts. Pour into individual star-shaped molds. Chill and serve on bed of lettuce topped with a swirl of whipped cream.

Lois McMillan
Bristow

LULA'S CRANBERRY SALAD

1 small pkg. cherry Jello
1 cup hot water
1 cup sugar
1 T. lemon juice
1 #2 can pineapple juice
1 cup ground raw cranberries
1 cup drained pineapple
1 cup chopped celery
½ cup chopped pecans

Dissolve Jello in hot water. Add sugar, lemon, and pineapple juices. Chill; stir remaining ingredients gently into chilled mixture.

Marian and Ken Childers
Bartlesville

Twenty years ago, after the Bob Mc-Cormicks got out of the service and returned to Oklahoma City from Hawaii, Peggy McCormick started making this coffee cake for Christmas morning.

DUTCH CHERRY CAKE

2 cups canned red cherries
½ cup flour
¼ tsp. salt
3 tsp. baking powder
¾ cup sugar
2 eggs, separated
½ cup milk
1 tsp. vanilla
½ cup shortening, melted

Drain cherries and save juice. Sift flour, salt, baking powder, and ½ cup sugar. Beat egg yolks and combine with milk, vanilla, and melted shortening. Add to flour all at once and beat with a spoon until smooth. Fold in cherries. Beat egg whites until stiff but not dry. Add remaining sugar, and fold into mixture. Bake in greased 7 x 11 x 1½ inch pan at 350° for 50 minutes. Then serve hot with cherry sauce. The batter may be mixed the night before and refrigerated. Then bake while the gifts are being opened.

CHERRY SAUCE

¼ cup sugar
2 T. flour
1 cup cherry juice
¼ cup butter
2 T. lemon juice
2 drops almond extract

Combine sugar and flour. Stir in cherry juice (reserved from cake) gradually. Heat to boiling and cook until thickened, stirring constantly. Add butter, lemon juice, and extract. Pour over cake. As it is served, it dribbles over the sides.

Peggy McCormick
Stillwater

"We have this coffee cake for Christmas morning brunch and give it to friends for the holidays, too."

COFFEE CAKE

1 pkg. yellow cake mix
1 pkg. instant vanilla pudding
¾ cup corn oil
1 stick butter
¾ cup water

4 eggs
1 tsp. butter extract
1 tsp. vanilla
¼ cup chopped nuts

FILLER

¼ cup sugar
¼ cup chopped nuts

2 tsp. cinnamon

GLAZE

1 cup powdered sugar
½ tsp. butter extract
½ tsp. vanilla
Enough milk to moisten

Grease bundt pan with entire stick of butter and sprinkle with ¼ cup chopped nuts. Put all cake ingredients into large mixing bowl and beat at high speed for 8 minutes. Alternate cake batter and filler in thirds into bundt pan. Bake at 350° for 40-45 minutes. Cool in pan for 8 minutes, then turn upside down on plate and add glaze. Delicious warm or cold. Freezes beautifully.

Betsy White
Oklahoma City

CHRISTMAS MORNING BREAKFAST

1 pound sausage
6 eggs
2 cups milk
1 tsp. salt
1 tsp. dry mustard
2 slices cubed bread
1 cup grated cheese

Brown sausage, drain, set aside. Beat eggs, add milk, salt, and mustard. Gently stir in bread and cheese, then sausage. Put in 8 x 12 inch buttered casserole. Refrigerate overnight. Bake at 350° for 45 minutes. Let sit for a few minutes before serving.

Serve with fresh fruit, your favorite coffee cake, and a glass of champagne.

Judy Jordan
Oklahoma City

As long as Phyllis Murray can remember, her family has looked forward to her mother's rolls on Christmas morning. They are so good and gooey that a fork is required.

MAMA'S CINNAMON ROLLS

1 cup sweet milk
¾ cup sugar
4 heaping T. shortening
1 tsp. salt
1 cake yeast
½ cup lukewarm water
1 egg, separated
6 cups flour, or more, as needed

Put yeast cake in lukewarm water to dissolve. Scald milk in double boiler, then add sugar, salt, and shortening. Cool to lukewarm and add dissolved yeast. Add 2 cups of sifted flour and yolk of egg. Beat white of egg until stiff and fold into dough. Add more flour and knead. Pour into a greased bowl and let rise about 2 hours. Refrigerate until ready to make up. (If plain rolls are desired, sugar can be decreased to ½ cup and dinner rolls shaped from this dough.)

To make the cinnamon rolls: In a large baking pan, pour enough melted margarine or butter to make a heavy coating. Sprinkle with brown sugar, dark Karo, and pecans.

Divide dough in half and roll out. Sprinkle with margarine or butter, white sugar, brown sugar, and cinnamon. Roll up and cut 1-inch slices. Place on top of pecan mixture in pan. (This recipe fills 1 large and 1 small pan.) These may be frozen at this point. If there is room in the refrigerator on Christmas Eve, let the rolls rise there overnight. Otherwise, remove from the freezer about 2 hours before baking on Christmas morning and let rise in the warm kitchen. Brush with melted butter and bake at 400° for 20 minutes or until nicely browned.

Mary Lelia Holmes
Norman

"It wouldn't be Christmas around our house if I didn't make at least two of these coffee cakes for Christmas breakfast. I usually make and form the cakes when we get home from Christmas Eve service and let them rise all night in a cold oven. The next morning I just bake them, and they are fresh from the oven—the house smells so good!

"The last few days before Christmas, I set aside time to make these for friends and neighbors as Christmas gifts. People tell me they save them for their Christmas breakfast, and it has become a tradition with them, too. All five of my children have helped, and their friends love to roll the dough in long strips and dip them in the cinnamon/sugar mixture. There is one rule, however; no coffee cakes for the Raineys until Christmas morning! This is very difficult for my four boys when there are coffee cakes all over the dining room table three or four days before Christmas. Some friends have received cakes with a strip removed from one end of the cake and the foil discreetly pulled over the missing piece! They tell me about this later!"

COFFEE CAKE

1 packet yeast
¼ cup warm water
¾ cup scalded milk
2 T. sugar
3 T. shortening
1½ tsp. salt
2½-3 cups sifted flour
1 stick butter

Soften yeast in the warm water. Combine the hot milk with sugar, shortening, and salt in a large mixing bowl. Cool to lukewarm and stir in yeast. Add flour gradually to form stiff dough. Knead on floured surface until smooth and satiny, about 3-5 minutes (or use dough hook in mixing bowl). Place in greased bowl and cover. Let rise in warm place until doubled, about 1 hour. Place a 15-inch sheet of aluminum foil, dull side up, on a cookie sheet (or, a pizza pan is perfect). Turn up the foil edges to form a 12-inch round "pan." Pinch off a little dough and roll into ½ inch thick by 6-8 inch long strips. Dip each strip in melted butter, then in cinnamon-sugar topping.

Start in the middle of the pan and make circular center of rolled dough. Each new dough section will encircle the dough placed down before. When all dough has been used, pour remaining topping over the cake. Cover and let rise in warm place about 1 hour. Bake at 350° for 25-30 minutes. When slightly cool, drizzle with icing made of ½ cup powdered sugar and 2 Tablespoons of milk.

Cont'd . . . .

CINNAMON SUGAR TOPPING

¾ cup sugar
¼ cup firmly packed brown sugar
2 tsp. cinnamon
¾ cup chopped nuts.

Combine all.

Edith Rainey
Edmond

"My grandmother, Stephanie Neugebaure, was German and made the most delicious bread for Christmas, which we always had for breakfast. She had no recipe, so I watched her make it and wrote down what she did."

STRITZEL

⅓ cup milk
1 tsp. sugar
1½ pkgs. dry yeast
1 stick butter
1 cup milk
4 eggs
½ cup sugar
½ cup raisins
2 tsp. anise
½ tsp. salt
3 cups flour, plus
1 egg, for glazing

Warm ⅓ cup milk and teaspoon of sugar, then add dry yeast. Leave in a warm place about 15 minutes, until foamy. Melt butter in 1 cup of milk and cool. In a large bowl, combine 4 eggs, ½ cup sugar, raisins, anise, salt, melted butter and milk. Add 2 cups of the flour and the yeast mixture, then another cup of flour. Stir with a wooden spoon, adding additional flour until you have a sticky dough. Knead in more flour for 10 minutes. Butter a large bowl, and place the dough in the bowl in a warm place covered with a damp cloth. Leave until the dough fills the bowl.

Butter a cookie sheet. Divide the dough into 4 pieces: 3 of them should be of equal size, and the 4th should be half again bigger than the 3 pieces. Braid the three pieces. Divide the large piece into 3 and braid them. Set the smaller braid on top of the larger one. Cover with a cloth and set in a warm place for 20-30 minutes. Brush bread with a whole beaten egg. Heat oven to 400°, and put bread in for 15 minutes. Reduce heat to 350° for 45 more minutes.

This bread is not good hot. It needs to cool and age a couple of days.

Bette Jo Hill
Oklahoma City

"Our father always went to our grandparents' home to cut a cedar tree down since they had a lot on their farm. He brought it home the day before Christmas Eve, and we decorated it with strings of popcorn and homemade ornaments, which were all we could afford. Each of us—there were 10 children—put an article of clothing under the tree so Santa Claus would know which one of us got which present. Then the lights were turned off, and Dad closed the door to the living room so we couldn't see in. We waited anxiously for a couple of hours for Santa Claus to arrive at our farm near Hennessey. Santa always came on Christmas Eve. Finally we were allowed to return to the tree and open the presents placed upon each piece of clothing. What a happy and exciting time for us!"

The favorite food handed down from Czech ancestors is Kolache, and Helen Shimanek Lamerton's mother always made them at Christmastime. Although the Shimanek family liked Kolaches best with poppyseed filling, prune and apricot fillings are also very popular. Czech Kolache Festivals each year at Prague and Yukon, Oklahoma, have made Kolaches a universal favorite with Oklahomans.

KOLACHES

1 cup milk
2 tsp. salt
6 cups flour
⅓ cup margarine
⅓ cup sugar
4 eggs, beaten well
1 cake yeast
¼ cup warm water

Scald milk. Cool to lukewarm. Dissolve yeast in warm water, add to warm milk. Add the sugar, salt, beaten eggs, and melted margarine. Mix. Add 3 cups flour, beat well, and let rise. Add remaining flour and work well. Place in greased bowl and let rise until double in bulk. Cut dough into small balls the size of golf balls and brush with melted margarine. Place in pan and let rise. Make indentation in each ball and fill with your favorite filling. Let rise a few minutes and bake at 350° about 20 minutes until brown. Brush with butter before removing from pan.

POPPYSEED FILLING

1 cup poppyseeds
¼ cup sugar
¼ cup milk
1 T. honey
1 tsp. vanilla
¾ tsp. grated lemon rind

Simmer all over low heat until thick.

Helen Lamerton
Edmond

94

LEMON BREAD

¼ cup milk
½ cup butter, melted
1 cup sugar
2 eggs
¼ tsp. almond extract
1½ cups sifted flour
1 tsp. baking powder
1 tsp. salt
½ cup nuts
1 T. lemon rind

Grease and flour a loaf pan. Cream butter and sugar. Beat in eggs one at a time. Add extract. Sift together dry ingredients, add alternately with milk. Blend together and add rind and chopped nuts. Pour into pan. Bake at 350° about 1 hour (or until crack forms in top).

LEMON TOPPING

¼ cup sugar
3 T. lemon juice

Mix together sugar and juice. While loaf is warm, drizzle over top, down sides, and into the crack.

For Christmas: Decorate the loaf by forming candied red cherries into flour petals. Cut candied green cherries into pieces to form leaves.

Eddi Morgan
Edmond

CRANBERRY BREAD

2 cups flour
½ tsp. salt
½ tsp. soda
1½ tsp. baking powder
1 cup sugar
1 orange
2 T. shortening
Boiling water
1 beaten egg
1 cup chopped pecans
1 heaping cup raw cranberries

Sift dry ingredients twice. To juice and grated rind of the orange, add the shortening and enough boiling water to make ¾ cup. Add beaten egg to dry ingredients, then orange juice mixture. Add nuts and cranberries. Mix and pour into greased bread pan. Bake at 325° for 1 hour.

Betty Hill
Oklahoma City

"John and I grew up in Lindsborg, Kansas, often referred to as 'Little Sweden, U.S.A.,' where Christmas Eve was always exciting with the traditional Smorgasbord served at home. Although we have lived many years and raised our family here in Oklahoma, the custom of our Swedish dinner on Christmas Eve is a very special time for all of us.

"A variety of appetizers are served buffet-style and must include pickled herring, knackebrod, Kumin Ost, and Bondost (Swedish cheese). The family gathers for the seated dinner at the dining table, centered with the old Swedish Christmas tree and candleabra surrounded by greenery. Delicacies include Potatiskorv (Potato Sausage), Kottbullar (Swedish Meatballs), Kalvstek (Veal Pot Roast), potatoes and gravy, vegetables, cranberry salad, Swedish Brown Bread, and, for dessert, Ostkaka (Curd Pudding) with ligonberries, whipped cream, and Swedish cookies.

"Swedish Brown Bread is a favorite year round, but at Christmas many loaves are baked for friends."

SWEDISH BROWN BREAD

1 cup quick oats
2 cups boiling water
2 T. shortening (rounded)
2 cakes yeast dissolved in lukewarm
  water
7-8 cups flour (enough to make very
  stiff dough)
2 tsp. salt
½ cup sorghum molasses
½ cup sugar

Pour boiling water over oats, shortening, salt, sorghum, and sugar. When lukewarm, add part of flour and mix. Then add the dissolved yeast, then more flour. Knead in thoroughly the remaining flour until the dough is stiff, but not sticky enough to stick to board. Let rise until double in bulk, put in two large loaf pans, and grease tops. Cover and let stand until double again. Bake at 350° for 45-55 minutes.

Shirley Winblad
Oklahoma City

"One of our favorite and most meaningful Christmas traditions is a family 'feast' on Christmas day prepared almost entirely by my mother-in-law. Turkey and all the trimmings are delicious, but her specialties are rolls and desserts: pies, cakes, fudge, and divinity. All are made lovingly and with great care. It always amazes me how Mina Lou can prepare this fabulous meal so effortlessly. It is always superb, and she takes great pleasure in her accomplishments! We love her for it!"

ORANGE STICKY ROLLS

6 cups flour
3 pkg. dry instant yeast
1 cup and 3 T. milk
¾ cup water
½ cup butter
⅜ cup sugar
1½ tsp. salt
2 eggs

Measure 2½ cups flour into large mixing bowl. Add dry yeast and blend. In a separate pan, measure milk, water, butter, sugar, and salt, and heat until just barely warm—stirring constantly. Pour into flour and yeast mixture. Add eggs and beat ½ minute at low speed, then 3 minutes at high speed. Gradually add rest of flour, mixing well. It will get too stiff for the mixer, so mix by hand until well mixed. Cover and let rise in a warm place. It doubles in about 45 minutes. It can be made into rolls at this stage or allowed to rise again until double, then worked down before making rolls. Place 2 Tablespoons of Orange Sauce in greased muffin tins. Then place roll in on top of the syrupy mixture. Let rise about 40 minutes and bake at 375° for 12-15 minutes.

ORANGE SAUCE

1 cup butter or margarine
½ cup brown sugar
½ cup frozen concentrated orange juice

Combine ingredients and cook over low heat until syrupy.

Ann Oswalt
Oklahoma City

"My mother and sisters would make at least 12 cakes and several pies at Christmas. When people dropped by during the holiday season in those days, they were offered cake with fruit juice or coffee. Large plates of cake and Christmas goodies were sent out to shut-in neighbors and less fortunate families who were not able to prepare for Christmas. My mother wanted the members of our immediate family to enjoy their favorite. Some liked chocolate, others lemon, but the majority's favorite was Coconut Cake. Usually four of the 12 would be coconut. The goal was to have plenty so that each one could enjoy his special cake or sample all.

"This fruit cake is quick, rich, and delicious, but not recommended for weight watchers. It does not require eggs, butter, sugar, flour, or baking powder. No brandy or wine is used, and it stays moist indefinitely."

WHITE FRUIT CAKE

2 cans Eagle Brand Milk
1 pound coconut, shredded
1 cup candied cherries
2 pounds dates
2 pounds nuts

Cut dates, chop nuts, and cut cherries in half. Mix all ingredients together. Lightly oil stemmed cake pan and line with wax paper. Pour in cake mixture and press VERY FIRMLY into pan. Bake at 325° for 25 minutes or until it sets. While warm, glaze with equal portions of dark Karo and canned apricot juice boiled together til thick. Before baking, decorate with candied fruits and nuts for Christmas.

Zella J. Patterson
Langston

These traditional Mediterranean pastries are usually prepared around Christmastime when large trays of sweets are served at gatherings of family and friends. This delight has gained in popularity in this country, and many of the Orthodox church women (both Lebanese and Greek) have bake sales open to the public either before the Thanksgiving and Christmas holidays or shortly before Easter. Baklawa is such a treat and so-o-o-o rich that it is served sparingly.

BAKLAWA ROLLS (LEBANESE)
BAKLAVA ROLLS (GREEK)

1 pound Baklawa Dough (fillo sheets
    carried at import shops)
1 pound pecans, chopped
½ cup sugar
1 tsp. Orange Water (import shop)
3 cups butter, rendered
1½ cups sugar syrup

Combine nuts and sugar together, add orange water, and stir. Set aside. With wide pastry brush, brush baking tray with melted butter. (To render butter, melt it and simmer until the butter clarifies and sediment forms. The oily part is rendered butter.) Work on wax paper; brush each sheet of dough generously with butter, placing one sheet on top of the other—using four sheets of dough.

Place nut mixture along wide edge. Fold ends over about 1 inch on each side; roll lengthwise. Place rolls in baking pan. Cut each roll on the angle into pieces the size you desire. (usually about 1½ inches thick). Dot with remaining butter. Bake in preheated oven at 250° until golden brown. Drain excess butter off completely, add cooled syrup.

SYRUP

2½ cups sugar
1½ cups water
1 tsp. lemon juice
1 tsp. Orange Blossom Water

Dissolve sugar in water and boil rapidly. Add Orange Blossom Water and lemon juice. Continue boiling until syrup resembles thin honey. *Cool* well before pouring over cooked Baklawa Rolls. This mixture can be prepared ahead of time.

Lynn Coury
Edmond

The Roosevelt Grill was an instant success when it opened in Edmond several years ago with its beautiful, but understated, decor and its exceptional continental menu. As its fame spread, many requests came in for catering, carry-outs, and luncheons. Hence the establishment of the Roosevelt Grill Pantry, which supplies the restaurant's pies, quiches, and cheesecakes and offers to the public all types of gourmet cookware, condiments, and prepared foods.

Alice Stammer, cook of many of the Grill's soups, patés, and sauces, is a partner in the pantry. Her recipe for Persimmon Pudding is a perfect steamed pudding for Christmas in Oklahoma where persimmons grow wild in the countryside and may be picked after the first freeze.

PERSIMMON PUDDING

1 cup persimmon pulp (uncooked)
2 eggs
1 cup sugar
1 cup flour
¼ cup sour milk
1 tsp. soda
1 tsp. cinnamon
1 tsp. nutmeg
1 tsp. vanilla
Pinch of salt
1 cup pecans or other nuts

Beat eggs thoroughly (no need to separate). Add pulp, sugar, and flour to which spices have been added. Add milk to which soda has been added (to get sour milk, 1 tsp. vinegar may be added to regular milk). Add nuts. Put into a buttered pudding mold or coffee can, about ⅔ full. Cover and set into a larger pot of water with a tight lid. Steam covered for 2 hours. Check for firmness. The pudding will still look moist but must be firm. (Note: Be careful taking the lid off as the steam can burn badly.)

Serve hot with Hard Sauce. The pudding may be doubled and may also be cooked in advance and reheated before serving, either by re-steaming or in a microwave. For a special Christmas treat, it is fun to flame the pudding on its serving platter by spooning warm brandy over it and then lighting. An alternate method is to pour lighted brandy over it. Slice to serve and add the Hard Sauce or pass it.

HARD SAUCE

1 cup sweet butter, softened
1 cup confectioners' sugar
¼ cup brandy, bourbon, or rum
Nutmeg

Cream the butter and sugar well. Add the brandy (rum flavoring may be substituted) a few drops at a time and beat until fluffy. Add the nutmeg to taste. Chill.

Alice Stammer
Edmond

100

MULBERRY PLANTATION LEMON MERINGUE CREAM

4 egg whites (room temperature)
½ tsp. cream of tartar
1 cup sugar
4 egg yolks
½ cup sugar
2 T. grated lemon rind
3 T. lemon juice
2 cups cream
1 T. sugar

Beat egg whites until frothy. Add cream of tartar and beat until they start to stiffen. Add the cup of sugar gradually, 2 Tablespoons at a time, and continue beating until meringue is glossy and stiff enough to hold its shape and spread on a lightly buttered 9-inch pie or cake pan. Make outside rim higher than middle. Bake in slow oven at 300° for 40 minutes.

While this is cooking, beat egg yolks until thick and lemon colored. Beat in ½ cup sugar, lemon juice, and rind. Cook in double boiler 15-20 minutes until thick. Cool. Whip 1 cup of the cream, fold into lemon mixture, blending thoroughly. Fill cooled meringue with this mixture and chill in refrigerator 8-16 hours. When ready to serve, top with 1 cup cream whipped with 1 Tablespoon sugar. Serves eight and is great!

Mrs. O. Alton Watson
Oklahoma City

CRANBERRY PUDDING

1 egg, beaten
¼ cup mild molasses
¼ cup light corn syrup
⅓ cup boiling water
1 tsp. soda
2 cups cranberries cut into ½ or ¼
1½ cups flour

Mix all ingredients. Grease and flour 1½ quart mold. Pour in batter. Cover tightly and steam 1½ to 2 hours.

SAUCE

1 cup sugar
½ cup cream
½ cup butter

Cook until thickened and serve warm over pudding.

Ethel Schraad
Edmond

Dinner by candlelight following Christmas Eve Communion at church is a new tradition for the Millar B. White, Jr. family. Betsy now wonders why they have not always done this, for Christmas day is much more relaxed with the tree in the morning and brunch afterward. It leaves the afternoon and evening for playing and visiting with friends, and nobody minds leftovers.

"My fondest memories of Christmas dinner include Ambrosia for dessert—we always had it—still do! I think it was because my Pappy thought it was necessary."

AMBROSIA

1 dozen oranges
Fresh coconut
½ cup sugar

Peel and section oranges. Crack, peel, and grate coconut. Mix together with sugar (Note: Some people use powdered sugar). Cover and keep in the refrigerator. Serve in stemmed glasses for a perfect Christmas dessert.

Betsy White
Oklahoma City

For as long as Gennie Johnson can remember, her family has served Sour Cream Raisin Pie for Christmas, from the time she was a girl in Chickasha until now as a mother with children of her own. Gennie has never seen the recipe in any cookbook and has considered it a well-kept family secret, but because it is such a Christmas tradition, she has shared her mother, Maidee LeForce's, recipe.

SOUR CREAM RAISIN PIE

1 cup raisins
1 cup sour cream
1 tsp. cornstarch
1 tsp. cinnamon
½ tsp. nutmeg
¼ tsp. salt
2 whole eggs plus 1 yolk
⅔ cup sugar

Put raisins in unbaked 8-inch pie shell. Blend other ingredients and pour over raisins. Bake at 450° for 10 minutes, then reduce to 325° and bake 25 minutes. Let cool. Cover with meringue and brown.

Gennie Johnson
Oklahoma City

"Our family's Christmas dinner has always been served in the afternoon after a morning of opening gifts. It always includes mincemeat pie. My great-grandmother made her own mincemeat from scratch, but my grandmother, Della Keef Harris, simplified the recipe by using prepared mincemeat. My mother still makes the best mincemeat pie in McAlester. Her pastry is flaky and light, but there is no recipe for that; she just adds ingredients until they look right!"

MINCEMEAT PIE

1 pkg. dried Nonesuch mincemeat
1 cup water
2 T. vinegar
2 T. strawberry preserves
2 T. sugar
1 tsp. butter

Mix all ingredients in a saucepan and bring to boil. Cook 1 minute. Cool. Place in an unbaked pie crust. Bake at 400° for 20-30 minutes.

PECAN PIE

3 eggs, beaten
1 cup white sugar
1 cup white Karo syrup
1 tsp. vanilla
Pinch of salt
¼ cup butter
l cup pecan halves

Beat eggs, add sugar, syrup, vanilla, and salt. Melt butter and add. Stir well, add pecans. Pour into unbaked crust and bake at 300° for 1 hour.

Linda Loveall Massad
Oklahoma City

No matter how delicious the mince-meat, pumpkin, or pecan pie filling, if the crust tastes like shoe leather the Christmas dessert is ruined! The secret is to avoid handling the pastry too much or rolling it out more than once.

AUNT NETTIE'S PIE CRUST

1 cup flour
⅓ cup shortening
½ tsp. salt
4-5 T. ice water

Sift flour and salt. Cut into shortening until very much like meal. Add ice water one spoonful at a time tossing gently.

Form into a ball and roll on floured board (or floured pastry cloth). Bake at 450° for 10-12 minutes, or fill and bake as required. This makes a one-crust pie, but can be successfully doubled for two-crust pies.

Susan Wade
Oklahoma City

When the young bride-to-be stepped off the boat from Germany, she could not speak a word of English and still had a long journey to Oklahoma Territory, where her *intended* had staked a claim in the Run of '89. Clara Schilling read and re-read the 54-page letter in which her fiance had outlined everything she must do to complete her journey. The train trip from New York to St. Louis was strange for the 18-year-old girl, but Charles Frost was there on the landing to meet her, and they married in St. Louis before continuing on to Oklahoma City where, for the first time, she saw the house he had built and furnished for her on East 7th. The year was 1906, and statehood was imminent. With it would come prohibition and the end of Frost's business, the distribution of 5 cent bottled beer.

Among the wonderful German treats Clara made annually at Christmas throughout her long life was a crispy, buttery cookie called Leopold Schnitten.

LEOPOLD SCHNITTEN

½ pound butter
1 cup flour
1 tsp. cinnamon
½ cup sugar
¼ pound grated unsalted almonds
½ tsp. allspice
Extra cinnamon/sugar mixture

Soften butter and cream with sugar well. Add flour, spices, and almonds. Press batter as thin as possible on sheet cake pan. Bake to light brown at 350° for 15-20 minutes. While hot, sprinkle generously with cinnamon/sugar. Cool slightly, cut into rectangles. Store in tins to keep crispy.

Marta Frost McGee
Edmond

MELTING MOMENTS

⅔ cup cornstarch
1 cup flour
1 cup butter
⅓ cup powdered sugar

Sift cornstarch and flour. Cream butter and sugar, then add dry ingredients. Drop by teaspoons in bite-sized amounts on ungreased cookie sheet. Bake at 325° for 15-20 minutes. Cool and frost with Lemon Butter Icing.

LEMON BUTTER ICING

Cream ¼ cup butter. Add 2 cups powdered sugar alternately with 2 Tablespoons of lemon juice. Stir in grated rind of 1 lemon. Add holiday touch with green or red food coloring.

Barbara Pannage Stanfield
Oklahoma City

Danish homes are filled with activity at Christmastime. Rooms are decorated with fir and candles, and housewives are busy with baking. Without home-baked cookies it would not be Christmas. When Helle Lykke married a young American doctor, Jim Males from Cheyenne, Oklahoma, and eventually moved to this country, she brought these Danish customs to her new home. Their two sons are teenagers and no longer hang stockings on the bedpost on "Little Christmas Eve" (two nights before Christmas) for candy and fruit, but the Males family continues to have a typical Christmas Eve feast and exchange gifts that evening.

Helle's friends love to sample the wonderful Danish cookies she makes every year. Pebbernodder is small, round, and about the size of a pigeon egg. The Males boys have sometimes followed the Danish custom of using the small cookies instead of coins when playing card games during the holidays. Each pebbernod represents the value of one "ore," the smallest coin in Danish currency.

PEBBERNODDER

1 cup butter
1 cup sugar
2 eggs
2½ cups flour
1 tsp. cardamon
1 tsp. cinnamon
¼ tsp. white pepper
Grated lemon rind

Sift dry ingredients into large mixing bowl. Add butter, eggs, and grated lemon rind. Mix well. Knead with hands until dough is smooth. Let rest 1 hour. Form small balls and bake on greased cookie sheet at 325° until golden brown, about 8 minutes.

BRUNE KAGER

1 cup butter
1 cup plus 3 T. sugar
3½ cups flour
¾ cup sorghum molasses
2 T. cloves
½ pound chopped almonds
½ tsp. ginger
3 tsp. cinnamon
1 T. grated orange rind
½ jar lemon and orange peel

Cream butter and sugar. Add rest of ingredients. Knead together. Form into 2 rolls and cool in refrigerator. Cut cookies very thin and decorate with half a split blanched almond. Bake at 325° for 8-10 minutes.

Helle Males
Edmond

106

TOFFEE BAR COOKIES

1 cup butter (½ & ½ margarine)
1 cup brown sugar
1 egg yolk
2 cups flour
1 tsp. vanilla
1 cup chopped pecans
12 ozs. Hershey Milk Chocolate Bar

Cream butter and sugar. Add yolk, vanilla, and flour. Spread thin with fingers on sheet cake pan. Bake at 350° for 10 minutes (til light brown). Meanwhile, melt chocolate slowly. Spread on baked cookie base while warm. Sprinkle with finely chopped nuts and press into chocolate lightly. Cut in rectangles when cooled but not hardened.

Linda Kennedy Rosser
Oklahoma City

As a special favor for her daughter, who is director of the Stephens County Museum at Duncan, Charlotte Jenkins' mother used the museum's collection of wooden cookie boards (or molds) to make Speculaas. The holiday cookies are kept tightly sealed through the year and brought out at Christmastime for exhibit. Some have been kept for over 15 years. (They are similar to gingerbread.)

SPECULAAS

3 cups flour
1½ cups butter, softened
½ tsp. baking powder
1½ cups brown sugar
3 tsp. cinnamon
1 tsp. cloves
1 tsp. nutmeg
¼ tsp. salt
A little milk if needed

Knead all ingredients together until they form a ball. Roll into individual balls of approximate amount for each mold. Chill. Dust mold with flour, and press dough in, leaving some excess at edges which can be cut off for a smooth border. Turn over and tap out onto a greased cookie sheet. LET COOKIES DRY AT ROOM TEMPERATURE 12-24 HOURS. Bake at 300° for 15 minutes until light brown. Remove to wax paper to cool. (If cookies are for hanging, make a hole near the top of the dough when half baked.) They can be frosted and decorated, or painted with acrylic paint.

Charlotte Jenkins
Duncan

Early in the Christmas season each year, hundreds of people flock to St. George Greek Orthodox Church for the annual Bake Sale, which features some of the most delectable Greek pastries, cookies, and breads anywhere. Many members of the church who do the baking are first-generation Greeks and very proud of the fine delicacies they create. Tom Lekas' mother is one of those, and now her daughter-in-law Sandra has learned to cook the Greek recipes. Although generally considered an Easter cookie, Koulourakia is the Lekas' family favorite and also is made at Christmas.

KOULOURAKIA

1 pound butter
2½ cups sugar
3 tsp. baking powder
6 eggs
1 tsp. vanilla
1 5½-oz. can evaporated milk
9-10 cups flour
Sesame seeds

Beat butter in mixer until really light colored. Then add sugar gradually and cream thoroughly. Add eggs one at a time and beat well. Stir in sifted dry ingredients and blend in flavoring. Knead well until dough is smooth. Pinch off pieces and roll into a snake, double over, and twist, making it about 3 inches long. For glaze, brush tops of cookies with mixture of 1 egg yolk and 2 Tablespoons water. Sprinkle with sesame seeds and bake at 350° for 15 minutes until lightly browned.

Sandra Lekas
Oklahoma City

Christmas Eve supper for the Ruth family in Geary was always Oyster Stew. On Christmas morning, there were always church services which the children attended reluctantly. "But it always gave us a good chance," recalls Helen Ruth, "to show off anything new in the clothing line we might have received." This sugar cookie recipe came from their father's home, which would make it well over 100 years old.

Cont'd . . .

108

PLAIN SUGAR COOKIES

1 cup sour cream
3 eggs
2 cups sugar
2½ cups flour
1 tsp. soda
1 cup butter or shortening
Pinch of salt

Cream butter and sugar. Add eggs. Sift flour, soda, and salt. Add alternately with sour cream. Drop by teaspoon on greased cookie sheet. Bake at 350° for 8-10 minutes until lightly browned. One cup of extra flour may be added if you wish to roll the dough for cutting. After baking, ice them and sprinkle with colored sugar.

Helen Ruth
Geary

DECORATED COOKIES

Use Helen Ruth's Plain Sugar Cookie recipe. Increase flour as suggested. Divide dough in half. Chill 1 hour until easy to handle. Roll out one half on a floured pastry cloth with rolling pin in floured pastry stocking. Roll to ¼ inch thickness. Cut with cookie cutters or use cardboard patterns as guides for cutting with a knife. Put on greased cookie sheet and bake in moderate oven (350°) about 10 minutes. Makes 2½ dozen moderate-sized cookies.

ICING

¼ cup butter or margarine
2 cups sifted confectioners sugar
1 tsp. vanilla
1 T. milk

Melt butter. Stir in sugar and milk gradually until smooth. Add vanilla. Divide into small portions and add various food colorings. Ice cookies in appropriate colors and, while icing is soft, sprinkle with colored sugar, red hots, miniature chocolate chips, silvers, or nonpareils.

Linda Kennedy Rosser
Oklahoma City

Since she was a teenager, Dorothy Kennedy has made Cocoa Fudge. At Christmas it was frequently mailed to aunts out of state. Her sweet tooth will not allow her to reserve the fudge for holiday time, however. It seemed that evening was when the irresistible urge to make fudge would come over her, to the delight of her daughter and son! Lee Kennedy has often said, "If Dorothy found out she had only 30 minutes to live, she would run in and make a batch of fudge."

COCOA FUDGE

⅔ cup Hershey's Cocoa
3 cups sugar
⅛ tsp. salt
1½ cups milk
¼ cup butter
1½ tsp. pure vanilla
1 cup pecans

Combine cocoa, sugar, and salt in a large saucepan. Add milk gradually. Mix thoroughly. Cook over low heat until sugar is completely dissolved, stirring gently occasionally. Turn up heat to medium high and bring to a rolling boil, stirring constantly. Reduce heat to medium and continue to boil without stirring until it reaches 232° F, or until small amount forms a soft, but firm ball, when dropped in a cup of cold water. (If using thermometer, be sure it is not resting on bottom of pan.) Remove from heat; add butter and vanilla, but DO NOT STIR! Cool at room temperature to 110° or lukewarm. While it cools, butter 8 x 8 x 2 inch pan. Add nuts and beat with wooden spoon until it thickens and loses some of its gloss. Quickly pour and spread fudge in pan. The more you beat the fudge, the more quickly it will harden. Cut into squares when cool. Be sure and give the pan to a nearby child to scrape! If no child is handy, an adult will like it just as well.

Dorothy Kennedy
Oklahoma City

PEANUT BUTTER CUPS

1 cup butter or margarine
1 cup peanut butter
1 pound powdered sugar
2 T. water
2 pounds semi-sweet chocolate summer coating

Mix first 4 ingredients well and form balls. Fill fluted paper candy cups ⅓ full with summer coating, melted in double boiler. Press in ball of peanut butter mixture. Add more chocolate on top. Let cool.

Margaret Fesler
Jones

110

"Sundial candy was a treat made by Aunt and Uncle John Sinopoulo, who came to Oklahoma before statehood. Their beautiful home on North Kelley, in Oklahoma City, which they named Sundial, is now our home. The candy was made for friends and loaded into Christmas baskets filled with homemade sausage, homegrown pears, Japanese persimmons, and pecans from our trees.

"More recently the Paul Dudmans, Stuart Careys, and Gambuloses celebrate Christmas three times: with a family dinner a week before with just the adults, Christmas Eve with all the little children at the Careys', and Christmas Day for everyone at the Dudmans'."

HONEY NOUGAT

3 cups white sugar
3 cups white Karo syrup
4 egg whites, stiffly beaten
½ cup honey, warmed
1 cup pecan halves

Combine sugar and syrup. Boil to 300°. Take from fire immediately and beat vigorously. Have stiffly beaten egg whites ready. Slowly add warmed honey to egg whites. Then pour egg white mixture slowly into cooled Karo and sugar mixture. Beat vigorously and add pecan halves. Pour into a buttered pan and cut into squares when cooled.

Pat Gambulos
Oklahoma City

"I have a new tradition every year, it seems, but the one thing I've done consistently for over 15 years is to make pecan toffee that is given to friends, neighbors, teachers, and co-workers."

PECAN TOFFEE

2 cups sugar
1 pound good butter
6 T. water
2 cups broken pecans
1 12-oz. bag semi-sweet chocolate chips*

*Many people use milk chocolate for Toffee.

Heat sugar, water, and butter in a heavy pan. Cook rapidly, stirring constantly until mixture reaches 295° on candy thermometer. Quickly add nuts and pour out on a buttered slab or foil-lined cookie sheets. When almost cool, brush with melted chocolate and put in cool place to harden. When cool, break into pieces.

Kitty Champlin
Oklahoma City

Almost since the beginning of their 25-year marriage, Margaret and Bill Wells have had a tradition that Bill furnishes the Peanut Brittle for the holidays. Using his mother's time-honored recipe, he assumed her tradition when he started a family of his own. The Wells family came to Oklahoma long before statehood, and his grandfather founded one of the earliest law firms in Oklahoma City.

Several years ago Bill decided to grow his own peanuts on country property he fondly calls the *Easy W Ranch.* Margaret's role in the Peanut Brittle tradition is to harvest and shell the peanuts! When the children were still at home, they frequently helped measure and stir and usually got the first samples after the crunchy confection finished hardening on the Wells' marble-topped breakfast table.

PEANUT BRITTLE

1 cup sugar
1 cup white Karo syrup
½ cup hot water
1 stick margarine
2 cups shelled raw peanuts
1 heaping tsp. baking soda

Using a heavy iron skillet, mix the sugar and syrup. Add the hot water and cook quickly on high heat, stirring, until the mixture threads. Reduce heat to medium low. Add the margarine. Melt. Add peanuts. Cook until the nuts brown, still stirring. Stir in soda. Pour out quickly on greased marble slab. Run a spatula underneath it. Pull the candy very thin when cool enough to handle.

Margaret and Bill Wells
Edmond

This fudge is made and shared with family and friends every Christmas by Dixie and George Day. Friends consider themselves lucky to be on their list when the delicious confection is delivered!

FIVE POUND FUDGE

4 ½ cups sugar
1 13-oz. can evaporated milk
¼ pound butter
1 jar marshmallow cream
12 oz. pkg. chocolate chips
12 oz. milk chocolate bar
2 cups chopped pecans
2 tsp. vanilla

Cook sugar, milk, and butter to soft ball stage, stirring. Take off heat and add remaining ingredients. There is no beating. Mix quickly and thoroughly. Pour into large rectangular glass casserole dish. Cool before cutting into squares.

Dixie and George Day
Edmond

Judy and Wes Morrison of Edmond spend one full evening together making Aunt Bill's Brown Candy for their friends at Christmastime. The recipe they use is from an old Mennonite Church cookbook from Geary, Oklahoma, where Wes grew up. The Morrisons have discovered the hard way that it is next to impossible to make this candy without four hands!

AUNT BILL'S BROWN CANDY

3 pints white sugar
1 pint whole milk (or cream)
¼ pound butter
¼ tsp. soda
1 tsp. vanilla
1 pound chopped pecans

Pour 1 pint of sugar into a heavy aluminum or iron skillet and place over a low fire. Begin stirring with a wooden spoon and keep the sugar moving so that it will not scorch at all. It will take almost half an hour to completely melt this sugar, and at no time let it smoke or cook so fast that it turns dark. It should be about the color of light brown sugar syrup.

As soon as you have the sugar started to heat in the skillet, pour the remaining 2 pints of sugar together with the pint of milk (or cream) into a deep, heavy kettle and set it over a low fire to cook along slowly while you are melting the sugar in the skillet.

As soon as all the sugar is melted, begin pouring it into the kettle of boiling milk and sugar, keeping it on very slow heat and stirring constantly. Now the real secret of mixing these ingredients is to pour a very fine stream from the skillet. Aunt Bill always said to pour a stream no larger than a knitting needle and to stir across the bottom of the kettle all the time.

Continue cooking and stirring until the mixture forms a firm ball when dropped into cold water. After this test is made, turn out the fire and immediately add the soda, stirring vigorously as it foams up. As soon as the soda is mixed, then add the butter, allowing it to melt as you stir. Now set off the stove, but not outdoors or in a cold place, for about 20 minutes, then add the vanilla and begin beating. Use a wooden spoon and beat until the mixture is thick and heavy, having a dull appearance instead of a glossy sheen. Add the broken pecan meats and mix. Turn into tin boxes or into square pans where it may be cut into squares when cooled slightly.

This keeps moist and delicious indefinitely and is most attractive when decorated with a sprig of holly, candied cherries, and halves of pecans.

Judy and Wes Morrison
Edmond

"We always have Divinity at Christmas. This recipe was my grandmother's, and she taught it to Mother, who passed it on to me. The secret is beating the egg whites until they are stiff and letting the mixture cook long enough THE SECOND TIME so that it crackles in the cold water."

DIVINITY

3 cups sugar
½ cup cold water
½ cup white Karo syrup
2 egg whites
1 tsp. vanilla
Pinch of salt
1 cup chopped nuts

Dissolve sugar, water, and Karo. Cook until it forms a soft ball. Slowly pour half of mixture over *STIFFLY* beaten egg whites, beating all the time with an electric mixer. Return remaining mixture to stove, and cook it until the syrup crackles in cold water. Add to the first mixture, beating, and add vanilla, salt, and pecans. (This is most successful if a heavy electric mixer is used, not a portable.)

Gay Reed
Oklahoma City

For many years the children in Susan Tague's family have made Orange Balls. Not only are they very easy to make, but easy to eat as well! Children love them. They are a cross between confection and cookies.

ORANGE BALLS

1 stick margarine
1 6-oz. can frozen orange juice
  concentrate, thawed
1 pound box powdered sugar
1 box vanilla wafers, finely crushed
Flaked coconut

Combine margarine, juice, sugar, and vanilla wafers. Roll into balls about the size of walnuts. Roll in flaked coconut. Freeze. Serve cold from the freezer.

Susan Tague
Oklahoma City

"When Dr. William Bennett Bizzell, President of the University of Oklahoma from 1925 to 1941, gathered his family together for Christmas in the old President's Home in Norman, a favorite treat was a special rich, creamy cocoa that was as traditional to the group as the turkey and fruitcake. Unlike any cocoa anywhere, its warmth and richness matched the warmth and richness of the occasion.

The cocoa, like the gathering of the entire family, remains a Thompson tradition and helps to recall those wonderful, old-fashioned Christmases of 40 and 50 years ago."

During the latter years of Dr. Bizzell's term, young grandchildren included were Carolyn (now Zachritz) and Ralph Thompson, now a Federal Judge, the children of Elaine Bizzell Thompson.

RECEPTION CHOCOLATE

1 cup dry cocoa
1½ cups sugar
1½ cups boiling water
¼ tsp. salt

Make a paste of these ingredients. Bring to a boil over flame; then cook 30 minutes in a double boiler. This is the basic paste for the drink, enough for 25 servings.

To Serve: Use ¾ cup paste and 1 cup whipped cream. In these proportions fold heavily whipped cream into paste. Mix 6 T. paste/cream, ½ tsp. vanilla, and 1 quart hot milk. One quart serves approximately 6 people.

Barbara and Ralph Thompson
Oklahoma City

JERRY'S EGG NOG

1 quart commercial egg nog
6 ozs. bourbon
2 ozs. rum
1 oz. brandy
½ pint whipping cream, whipped

Mix all and serve very cold. To increase, 7 quarts will make a total of 3 gallons and serves at least 35 people.

Betty Ann Furseth
Oklahoma City

Families who have been special to Mary and Rowland Denman and their daughters, Beth and Amy, through the year are invited to their home in Edmond on Christmas aftrnoon for Egg Nog and Milk Punch. Rowland first tasted Milk Punch, a very traditional Southern drink, when he was a student at Washington and Lee University in Virginia, and the recipe has become a tradition for the Denman family in Oklahoma.

MILK PUNCH

3 oz. milk
2 tsp. sugar
1½ oz. half & half
1½ oz. bourbon
¼ tsp. vanilla

Shake with cracked ice. Strain and chill.

(Multiply accordingly). When ready to serve, pour over fresh cracked ice in highball glasses and dust with nutmeg.

Mary and Rowland Denman
Edmond

GINGERBREAD HOUSE

6 cups sifted flour
4 tsp. ground ginger
1 cup butter or margarine
1 cup light brown sugar
½ cup dark corn syrup
½ cup light molasses

Sift flour before measuring. Measure, then sift again with ginger into larger bowl. In medium saucepan combine 1 cup each butter or margarine and light brown sugar (firmly packed), corn syrup, and molasses. Heat over low heat, stirring occasionally until butter melts. Stir into flour mixture, then beat well until blended. Cool dough 5 to 10 minutes. While still warm for easier handling, divide dough in half and roll out for cutting (directions for size and assembly to follow). When pieces are cut, place on cookie sheet and chill before baking to hold shape. Preheat oven to 375° and bake pieces 18-20 minutes or until edges are lightly browned and center is dry to touch. Remove smaller pieces, such as shutters, after 5-8 minutes baking time. Cool pieces on cookie sheet on wire rack for 5 minutes. Loosen carefully and remove to wire rack for complete cooling before assembly.

Cont'd . . .

DECORATOR'S FROSTING SNOW

3 egg whites
⅛ tsp. cream of tartar
1½ (16 oz.) pkgs. confectioners sugar

In medium bowl with electric mixer at medium speed, beat egg whites and ⅛ tsp. cream of tartar until frothy, then beat in confectioners' sugar a Tablespoon at a time. Beat until very stiff and mixture does not flow together when cut through with a knife.

HOUSE PATTERN AND ASSEMBLY

Make cardboard or paper patterns. For front of house, draw 8½ x 8 inch rectangle and cut out. Fold in half lengthwise; then cut a triangle from one end for roof pitch. For the windows, cut out 1½ x 1 inch rectangle about 1¾ inches from bottom and right side. For top window cut out 1 inch square 2 inches from peak of roof.

For back of house, make pattern like the front but omit the windows. For sides, draw two 6¼ x 5 inch rectangles and cut out. For door, draw 3¼ x 2 inch rectangle and cut out. For shutters, draw two 1 x ⅝ inch rectangles and two 1¼ x ¾ inch rectangles and cut out. For scalloped roof trim, trace top of house front on paper, extending each side 1 ¼ inches. Starting from center, draw scallops, about ¾ inch deep.

Cut out two of them.

For roof, cut two 5 ¾ inch squares. Make chimney cutout on one square (the roof will be made from the dough, then covered with cookie shingles). For canopy over front door, cut two 2 x 1½ inch rectangles. Cut out all pieces, bake, and cool according to gingerbread instructions. Gingerbread man and woman, as well as trees and other accessories, may be cut from this dough with standard cookie cutters.

Assembly: It is easiest to decorate pieces BEFORE asembling the house while they can be laid flat; then allow all decoration to set well before putting the house together.

Cont'd . . .

1 pkg. coconut bar cookies
Peanut candy (for chimney)
2 chocolate wafer cookies
Boston Baked Bean candy
Red hots
Unsweetened chocolate, melted
Green gumdrop wreaths
Coconut (dry, flaked)

Spread top half of well-cooled front piece with Frosting Snow, spreading smoothly. Pipe chocolate for timbered effect. With small spatula, spread shutters with icing and set in place (this icing will serve as "glue"). Decorate front door by coloring small amount of icing with red food coloring; paint the front door with this. Attach several red hots to gumdrop wreath, then place on front door. Spread back of door with frosting and set against front of house, slightly ajar. Then do the same with chocolate wafer window box filled with red hot "flowers" and green gumdrop "leaves." Canopy over front door should then be secured with frosting.

Top half of other three sides of house should be spread with frosting and piped with timbered effect like the front.

Allow all four sides to dry thoroughly. To cement house together, slowly melt one cup of white sugar in a heavy skillet until it looks caramel colored. Work quickly but CAREFULLY with this as it hardens fast *and can burn the skin.* (An alternative cement is frosting made exactly like the Frosting Snow except with only 1 egg white and rolled in pencil strips like putty. However, this does not hold as well or as permanently as the melted sugar.)

Stand up one side-wall with inside against one or two unopened fruit or soup cans. Spoon hot sugar along edge of second side and press one gabled end of house at right angles to edge with cement. Again, use a can for support. Repeat with remaining walls. Messy seams can be hidden with frosting later. Let the frame set for 30 minutes until firm. Remove cans and place roof pieces on with sugar cement. Place cookies on roof as shingles, going from bottom to top and leaving space for chimney on one side, using the frosting snow as glue. Build chimney out of peanut square candy, using frosting snow as mortar. Decorate roof with frosting snow and coconut. Decorate yard with snow, coconut, and rock path of Boston Baked Bean candy.

The best kind of base is a wooden cutting board, a piece of pressed board, or plywood. The house can be frozen for at least five years and used annually.

Linda Kennedy Rosser

BIBLIOGRAPHY

Berry, Becky, "Grandma Berry's Ninety Years in Oklahoma," *Chronicles of Oklahoma*, XLV, 1967.

Blackwell Times Record, December 26, 1912.

Campbell, O.B. *Tales They Told* (Oklahoma City: MetroPress, 1977).

Chapman, Berlin Basil. *The Founding of Stillwater* (Oklahoma City: Times Journal Publ. Co., 1948).

Cheyenne Transporter, December 26, 1881; December 26, 1891.

Chicago Tribune, January 21, 1885.

Daily Oklahoman, December 22, 25, 1907.

The Duncan Banner, December 19, 1979; December 4, 1981.

The 1889ers, *Oklahoma, The Beautiful Land* (Oklahoma City: Times-Journal Publ. Co., 1943).

El Reno News, December 23, 1893.

Gibson, Arrell M., *The Oklahoma Story* (Norman: University of Oklahoma Press, 1978).

Grierson, Col. B.H., "Grierson Letters" (Mss., Reference Library, Oklahoma Historical Society, Oklahoma City).

House, R. Morton, "The Only Way Church and the Sac and Fox Indians," *Chronicles of Oklahoma*, XLIII, 1965.

The Indian School Journal, 1905-1906 (Reference Library, Oklahoma Historical Society, Oklahoma City).

King, C. Richard, ed., *Marion T. Brown: Letters From Fort Sill, 1886-1887* (Austin: The Encino Press, 1970).

Kingfisher Free Press, December 13, 1900.

"Kiowa Field Matron Reports," (Archives & Manuscript Division, Oklahoma Historical Society, Oklahoma City).

Letter Book, Adjutant General's Office, January 15, 1885, Vol. LXXIV.

Morris, John W., Goins, Charles R., and McReynolds, Edwin C., *Historical Atlas of Oklahoma* (Norman: University of Oklahoma Press, 1976).

Oklahoma City Times, December 25, 1947.

Oklahoma War Chief, April 15, 1886.

Oswego Democrat, December 22, 1911.

The Ponca City News, December 2, 1976; November 27, 1979.

Rister, Carl Coke, *Land Hunger* (Norman: University of Oklahoma Press, 1942).

Shirk, George H., *Oklahoma Place Names* (Norman: University of Oklahoma Press, 1974).

Tulsa Daily World, December 22, 1929; December 21, 1930.

Works Progress Administration, "Indian and Pioneer History," Vol. XLII (Archives & Manuscript Division, Oklahoma Historical Society, Oklahoma City).

Wright, Muriel H., *The Story of Oklahoma* (Oklahoma City: Webb Publishing Co., 1929-30).

RECIPE INDEX